When the Lion Roars

D0043265

When the Lion Roars

a primer
for the
unsuspecting
mystic

Stephen J. Rossetti

ave maria press Notre Dame, Indiana

Scripture texts used in this work are taken from *The New American Bible* copyright © 1991, 1986, and 1970 by the Confraternity of Christian Doctrine, Washington, DC, and are used by permission of the copyright owner. All rights reserved. No part of *The New American Bible* may be reproduced in any form or by any means without permission in writing from the publisher.

Excerpts from *The Collected Works of Saint John of the Cross*, trans. by Kieran Kavanaugh and Otilio Rodriguez, copyright © 1979 by the Washington Province of the Discalced Carmelites, Inc. Reprinted by the permission of ICS Publications.

Excerpts from *Four Quartets* by T. S. Eliot, copyright © 1971, used by permission of Harcourt, Inc.

Excerpts from *The Wisdom of the Desert* by Thomas Merton, copyright ©1960 by the Abbey of Gethsemani, Inc. Reprinted by the permission of New Directions Publishing Corp.

Nihil Obstat:

Rev. Joseph Zareski
Censor Deputatus

Imprimatur:

Most Rev. James M. Moynihan
Bishop of Syracuse, NY
Given at Syracuse, NY, on September 23, 2000

© 2003 by Ave Maria Press, Inc.

All rights reserved. No part of this book may be used or reproduced in any manner whatsoever, except in the case of reprints in the context of reviews, without written permission from Ave Maria Press, Inc., P.O. Box 428, Notre Dame, IN 46556.

www.avemariapress.com

International Standard Book Number: 0-87793-985-3

Cover and text design by Katherine Robinson Coleman

Printed and bound in the United States of America.

Library of Congress Cataloging-in-Publication Data

Rossetti, Stephen J., 1951-
When the lion roars : a primer for the unsuspecting mystic / Stephen J. Rossetti.
    p. cm.
Includes bibliographical references (p.   ).
    ISBN 0-87793-985-3 (pbk.)
1. Mysticism. 2. Mystics. I. Title.

BV5082.3 .R67 2003
248.2'2--dc21

2002152566
CIP

The lion roars—

who will not be afraid!

The Lord God speaks—

who will not prophesy!

Amos 3:8

To Andrew J. Rossetti

1982-2001

Come my friends,

  'Tis not too late to seek a newer world.

Push Off, and sitting well in order smite

The sounding furrows; for my purpose holds

To sail beyond the sunset, and the baths

 Of all the western stars, until I die.

 It may be that the gulfs will wash us down;

 It may be we shall touch the Happy Isles,

 And see that the great Achilles, whom we knew.

 Tho' much is taken, much abides; and tho'

 We are not now that strength which in the old days

 Moved earth and heaven, that which we are, we are,—

  One equal temper of heroic hearts,

 Made weak by time and fate, but strong in will

To strive, to seek, to find, and not to yield.

       Alfred Tennyson, "Ulysses"

Contents

	Introduction	8
1.	Purely a Gift	11
2.	Intoxicated on God's Milk	15
3.	Ever More the Beginner	20
4.	Friends of God	24
5.	Facing Sin Is Freedom	29
6.	Judge Not	34
7.	The Need to Be Guided	40
8.	Living for God Alone	46
9.	Thy Will Be Done	51
10.	Waiting	56
11.	God Is the Present	60
12.	Pray Always	65
13.	Praying Is Breathing	70
14.	Munching on Jesus	75
15.	The Scriptures Are Our Consolation	81
16.	Ecstasies Are a Distraction	85
17.	Flee From Locutions	89
18.	Seek Mercy, Not Suffering	95
19.	Knowing by Not Knowing	100
20.	Safe Harbor From Evil	106
21.	Our Radiantly Humble God	111
22.	The Sound of God	117
23.	The Noisy Distractions of Humanity	122
24.	Bearer of God's Joy	129
25.	Bearers of God	135
26.	A Life Hidden in the Triune God	141
27.	In the End Is My Beginning	147
	Notes	153
	Selected Bibliography	157

Introduction

A Christian mystic is first of all a Christian,
but what is *implicit* in the Christian life becomes,
in the mystic, *explicit*.

CHRISTIANITY CANNOT SURVIVE IN THIS WORLD, OR IN OUR
own lives, without its mystical roots. In this sense, mysticism is not the reception of extraordinary, miraculous
experiences. Rather, the mystic is one who is fully alive in
a vibrant relationship with God. The mystic's God is not
a distant, foreboding power, but the Intimate One who is
here and now.

Our hearts yearn and indeed, *demand*, a dynamic
"now" relationship with God. We were meant for such an
intimacy. We will taste something of the mystical life in our
day or else our faith, trying to exist in this barren world,
will dry up. It is not so much that mystics have something
that others do not. Rather, they are beacons pointing each
of us to a divine intimacy that God offers to all.

I have met such beacons in my life. I remember well a
hermit who was such a beacon for me. I also remember an
older married woman who showed me something of the
face of God. And I recall a kind and gentle pastor who
likewise helped to point the way. It is clear to me that each
of them was fed daily on the bread of God. They were
slowly transformed as they inhaled the breath of God.
Divine life flowed through them and, many times, radiat-
ed from their faces and in their eyes. They had a joy and

peace that I found inviting. Their mystical roots kept them steady, even in times of great suffering.

It was not my intention to write this book. Speaking of the mystical life in prose is impossible. By its very nature, a direct experience of God is beyond words. Such a truth is better expressed in poetry, art, music, and symbol, although the very best approach to mysticism is a reverent silence. To stand before God, and in God, stuns the soul into silence. What wells up in the heart seems deflated when put into words.

But an inspiration touched me one day, of all times, while getting a haircut. A simple thought passed into my heart: I should write a book. It would be a book that speaks to people of today about the mystical life. I would share with them something of the wisdom of the great masters of this life. Indeed, I have been nourished by their words, and most importantly, I have shared in their spirit, which is very much alive even now. Perhaps it was they who spoke to me that day.

Subsequently, I dismissed the thought to write a book. But it surfaced again and again, with an increasing insistency. In fact, it began to be a constant "note" sounding in the recesses of my consciousness. I recalled the words of Saint Paul who said, "for an obligation has been imposed on me, and woe to me if I do not preach it!" (1 Cor 9:16). So, too, I knew that God would not let me rest until I had finished this book. Now, it is finished.

Nevertheless, it was a daunting task conveying the complexity and yet stunning simplicity of the life of the Spirit. But there were so many times that, in the writing of these chapters, I became filled with a powerful emotion. I was overcome with the loving immensity of God. "O Bonitas!" as the hermit and mystic Bruno would often exclaim. O what goodness is our God! See how the Lord blesses us when we do the divine bidding.

I would like everyone to be filled with this wonder. I would like everyone to know and to be filled with the goodness of our God. In the pages to come, I will speak of the simple truth that God is with us. The divine presence fills all of creation and every corner of our lives.

By convention I will speak sometimes of God using a masculine pronoun. While God is beyond human gender, the mystical life is incredibly personal and demands the use of personal pronouns. Unfortunately, our language is limited. But what must be communicated is an intimacy with the divine that is immediate, overwhelming, and personal.

To be alive, to be a passionate Christian today, is to be a mystic, someone who has been blessed directly and profoundly by the immediate intervention of God. If you have not been so blessed, read on. There must be a reason why God has placed this book in your hands. If you have received such graces, I hope that this little book is of some help as you try to navigate the sometimes treacherous waters of grace and delusion, of mysticism and madness.

In the end, the life of the Christian mystic is profoundly simple: give thanks always. Pray constantly. And let the words of Bruno well up in your heart as you cry out, "O Bonitas!" O what a wonderful God!

One

Purely a Gift

THIS BOOK IS FOR AND ABOUT MYSTICS, CHRISTIAN MYSTICS. BY "mystic," I do not mean someone who necessarily has had extraordinary supernatural experiences, although these sometimes do occur. Nor am I speaking of those who claim to possess a hidden knowledge of a secret spiritual realm. Rather, Christian mystics are those who live the Christian life "with the gloves off." What is often implicit in the life of Christians is revealed more plainly in the mystics. These men and women experience directly and powerfully the dynamic and overwhelming Truth. And they can say without hesitation, as did the prophet Amos, that the Lion has roared.

This may seem like a pretty rarefied group. After all, how many authentic mystics are there in the world today? Does our faith not tell us that there is no new public revelation of God after the revelation that was Jesus? Indeed, there is no need for any additional *public* revelation;

Jesus is the complete revelation of God. Everything that can and needs to be said about God has been said in the person of Jesus. So, why should we put any credence in the idea that God continues to reveal himself?

The answer lies in the sheer overflowing generosity of God. It is the divine generosity that gives rise to the plethora of *private* revelations today. My experience listening to people today is that one could easily argue that God is revealing himself as often and as powerfully today as at any time in human history. The scriptures tell us that our God gives in abundance: "a good measure, packed together, shaken down, and overflowing, will be poured into your lap" (Lk 6:38). It is the very nature of God's boundless love to overflow the heavens and to shower blessings upon us. It would be contrary to God's very nature for the flowing waters of divine self-revelation to dry up. God cannot *not* bless us! And there is no greater blessing that God can bestow than letting us taste his very self. God's best and greatest gift is himself.

God wants all of us in every walk of life to taste the divine goodness. God wants to share with us everything that is his. It is the divine will that we be completely taken up into God's overwhelming joy: "I have told you this so that my joy might be in you and your joy might be complete" (Jn 15:11). God wants us to be one with him.

Mystics are not part of a small, elite society that has attained some special status by its own work. *Rather, mystics are people who have come to experience the intense, personal desire God has to share himself with us*: "I have eagerly desired to eat this Passover with you" (Lk 22:15). That Passover meal is himself. Jesus longed to share his very self with the disciples.

Mystics achieve nothing by their own merits; they have simply learned to fix their gaze upon the Lord and to open their hearts to his boundless goodness. If their hearts are full of joy and their eyes radiate a spiritual light, it is because the Lord himself has done this. It sounds incredibly simple . . . and it is.

Disappointed? Naaman, the army commander of Aram, asked for a special grace from the prophet Elisha to cure his leprosy. Naaman was expecting to be told to do something unusual or difficult. He was advised, however, only to wash seven times in the Jordan River. He was angered at the advice. He expected something much more difficult, and so he left the prophet's presence believing that his petition had not been granted. But his servants pleaded with him, "If the prophet had told you to do something extraordinary, would you not have done it? All the more now, since he said to you, 'Wash and be clean,' should you do as he said" (2 Kgs 5:13). He washed in the Jordan and he was made whole.

If you are looking for some secret recipe or special exercise that will turn you into a mystic, you will be disappointed. If you are seeking a special secret way, your desire is for magic, not Christian mysticism. There is no special mantra, no magic place, and certainly no meditation technique that automatically brings down the divine presence. This search for "the mystical secret" is a recurring temptation for every would-be guru and the error of many who desire to travel this road. God is not a divine slot machine that gives out the coins of grace when the right numbers appear.

God is a divine person who sheds his love freely and without cost. God's voice reverberates throughout creation proclaiming his invitation:

> All you who are thirsty,
> come to the water!
> You who have no money,
> come, receive grain and eat;
> Come, without paying and without cost,
> drink wine and milk! (Is 55:1)

It seems so simple, and it is simple. But it is a divine simplicity that takes a lifetime, and maybe more, for weak humans to enter. As the mystic Therese of Lisieux

exclaimed, "Everything is a grace!"[1] Learning to accept
the utter gratuity of grace is abhorrent to us. Such a completely undeserved gift places us totally in God's debt.
And it tells us clearly that we are creatures and he is the
Creator.

Can you stand, for even a brief moment, to let go of
control? The magician controls the illusion, but the mystic abandons all human control to be open to the Other.
This, too, is a message that is easy to accept in theory, but
one that takes a lifetime to learn in practice. Such humility requires a complete transformation.

God is boundless generosity. Tasting God is purely a
gift. We only need to open our hearts and hands to receive
this gift. This is the first lesson and it is the last lesson. If
you take in nothing else, this is enough. Read this simple
chapter many times. Read it again and again. Learn it;
meditate upon it. As the days pass and you travel farther
down the mystical road, the words will ring truer with
each passing year. A good sign of authentic progress on
this path is to recognize more fully, with each passing day,
this truth: all is grace; all is God's gift.

two

Intoxicated

on God's Milk

BEGINNERS ON THE MYSTICAL ROAD USUALLY START WITH A
kind of honeymoon period. God often showers blessings
and consolations on the beginner in considerable
abundance. It is a time of intense spiritual fervor and can
inaugurate a powerful "second conversion." The first
conversion is the acceptance of faith and a desire to lead
a Christian life. The second conversion is a decision to
walk the "narrow path," a dedication of one's self to live
directly and totally for God.

During the time of consolations, one comes to recognize that all is "straw" compared to the beauty and
grandeur of God, as Thomas Aquinas learned in his own
mystical experience. Toward the end of his life, Thomas

received a powerful revelation and subsequently said,
"All that I have written appears to be as so much straw
after the things that have been revealed to me."[2] Indeed,
compared to God, human works are so much straw.

Beginning the spiritual journey is a time of a new
awareness of God. It is a time full of promise. It begins an
explicit walking of the path toward union with God. Like
the newly married couple, there are often many moments
of bliss and an experience of a love that is boundless.
Indeed, the beginning of the mystical life is often a special
time of consolations in which God seems particularly
generous in bestowing special graces on the mystical
neophyte.

But beginners, being showered with God's consolations, almost always have a distorted view of themselves
that may be increasingly filled with spiritual hubris or
pride. John of the Cross, the "mystical doctor," said the
conduct of beginners in the spiritual journey is "very
weak and imperfect . . . their motivation for their spiritual works and exercises is the consolation and satisfaction
they experience in them." They may nurture a "secret
pride." He added that they become judgmental: "In their
hearts they condemn others who do not seem to have the
kind of devotion they would like them to have."[3]

Early in the mystical path, when we are filled with
consolations and special graces, it is common to develop
this spiritual pride. We may judge others' spirituality and
find them wanting. We secretly believe that we are wonderfully spiritual persons who are very close to final
union with God. We may even have a desire to teach
others the "right" way, even those who have walked the
spiritual path for many years. Beginners are full of fervor
and their enthusiasm is a great gift for everyone. But their
spiritual arrogance can be tiresome.

The beginning of the mystical path also carries with it
some unique dangers. In the beginning, everything spiritual and ascetical seems easy. The beginner may take on
significant penances and may even engage in more

extreme forms of asceticism. This can be dangerous to the body, the mind, and the spirit.

When people begin the spiritual journey, they almost never have a balanced view of the place of ascetical practices. They, as yet, do not realize in their hearts that the consolations they are experiencing are purely a grace. Beginners are prone to believe that if they live an ascetical and pure life, these consolations will continue, perhaps even increase. And, in the midst of consolations that place the body, psyche, and spirit in a state of euphoria, ascetical practices do not seem difficult and may actually be welcome.

This is a normal state for beginners. Yet, it can also be quite dangerous. The most dangerous part of all is that beginners, as part of their spiritual egotism, may set themselves up as their own teachers and guides. Thus, they may blindly charge ahead unchecked.

What should novice mystics do? The first step is to give thanks for this special time of consolation and for the generosity that God is showing. In addition, we must begin to take in the truth that God's grace is purely a gift, completely gratuitous. It is not a reward for anything we have done. Nor can it be bought by ascetical practices.

The second step is to try to accept the fact that this time of consolation, as wonderful as it is, is the "milk" of God and not "solid food" (Heb 5:12-13). The milk is exhilarating and an important part of the journey. But its presence should tell us that the journey is just beginning, not almost ending. We do not eschew these special graces, nor should we become too attached to them. But it is, indeed, difficult not to become too attached to the milk of God. It is very intoxicating. Perhaps it is for this reason that it will disappear soon enough.

The truth comes to the fore when these early consolations disappear. As John of the Cross teaches us:

> It should be known, then, that God nurtures and caresses the soul, after it has been resolutely converted to His service, like a loving mother who

warms her child with the heat of her bosom, nurses it with good milk and tender food, and carries and caresses it in her arms. But as the child grows older, the mother . . . sets the child down from her arms, letting it walk on its own feet so that it may put aside the habits of childhood and grow accustomed to greater and more important things.[4]

When the milk is withdrawn, some beginners become angry. They are angry at God and may abandon the spiritual life altogether. Clearly, their motive in following the mystical path was the consolations they received, that is, what they were getting out of it. But one cannot follow the mystic path with such self-centered aspirations. In the end, we must focus our eyes on God. Our delight must be in fulfilling his will. Letting go of self to focus on another may be difficult for many in our narcissistic age.

Other beginners, once the milk of God's consolations is withdrawn, may grasp for control; that is, they may try to recapture the "right" external circumstances so that the consolations will return. They may go back to the sites where the graces were first received. They may try to remember the prayers they were praying or what they were doing when they first received God's favor. Unfortunately, these efforts are futile and only exacerbate their frustration.

Others may take the withdrawal of God's milk as a sign of personal failure. They may scan through their lives trying to figure out what sin they had committed. Or they may double their ascetical efforts assuming that they have not been "holy enough" to merit more consolations. These people are likely to become downcast and discouraged.

At such a moment, a wise spiritual director can be a life-saving grace.[5] Also, grieving the loss of God's milk would be appropriate. It is good for people to mourn the loss of their childhood as they move into adulthood. Our spiritual childhood was a wonderful time. We grieve its loss and we give thanks for the graces received.

Most of all, we must learn the prayer of trust. God will surely lead us. We must learn to trust his lead. This is the spiritual insight contained in the mystical work by Jean-Pierre de Caussade. He wrote that true holiness means:

We lovingly accept all that God sends us at each moment of the day . . . we accept what very often we cannot avoid, and endure with love and resignation things which could cause us weariness and disgust.[6]

Thus, we move forward. We are confident in whatever comes our way, whether it be directly or indirectly from the hand of God. Even if what comes our way is evil, we know that God can make good come of it: "We know that all things work for good for those who love God" (Rom 8:28).

In the midst of consolations, we feel very holy and very special. But when the milk of God disappears and we "return to earth," we feel a bit humbled and very ordinary. Thank God that we are brought back to earth, lest we be swallowed up in our spiritual pride! A drop of humility and a sense of our frail humanity are more salvific than any sweet consolation.

Once the milk of God has been withdrawn, the novice is now ready to begin the mystical journey in earnest.

three

Ever More

the Beginner

HAVING TASTED GOD'S MILK AND GIVEN THANKS, WE MAY FEEL immediately desirous of preaching to others or heading off on a personal crusade to change the world. This is almost always a misguided impulse.

Paul of Tarsus, after having had his mystical experience, spent three years in the desert in spiritual preparation. Initially, he had been struck blind by an overwhelming experience of the risen Lord. He wandered into Damascus as a blind man until a member of the Christian community, Ananias, laid hands on him (Acts 9:1-19). His public ministry began only after a long period of preparation in the desert, a time of three years. Similarly, Catherine of Siena, another great mystic, spent three years in solitude and prayer before engaging in public works. At the end of her hermit period, she was mystically espoused to Christ and heard the call to serve the poor in Siena.

Launching out on a personal spiritual crusade at the beginning of one's mystical journey is almost always a sign of spiritual pride. John of the Cross tells us that beginners "develop a desire somewhat vain—at times very vain—to speak of spiritual things in others' presence, and sometimes even to instruct rather than be instructed."[7]

Once touched by an overwhelming experience of God, it is a natural impulse to desire sharing this wonderful news with others. The grace of God very often carries with it the desire to communicate to others. Indeed, the beginner may engage in sharing this newfound enlivened faith with others, but not as a teacher, and certainly not as a spiritual director. Instead of teaching, one should become a learner.

And what the beginner embarks upon is not so much learning new ideas about God, although this may happen, but the mystical journey imparts a different kind of knowledge. *To set forth on the mystical journey is to begin a whole new way of knowing.*

These earliest mystical graces open the door to a deeper kind of learning about God. In his masterpiece, *The Degrees of Knowledge*, the philosopher Jacques Maritain speaks of many different levels of knowledge. Our senses give us some forms of knowledge; our intellect teaches us other truths. But Jacques Maritain noted that the highest form of knowledge occurs in "mystical contemplation." In this state, one learns about God directly through a "supernatural connaturality." The mystic learns through a loving union with God the deep truths of who God is.[8]

When the mystical door is opened, what is learned and experienced is beyond speech. Mystics grasp for symbols or metaphors. They may be moved to poetry or song, since these artistic forms of expression are more able to express the unspeakable Truth than prose. I am reminded of the beautiful poetry of John of the Cross:

How gently and lovingly
You wake in my heart,
Where in secret You dwell alone;
And by Your sweet breathing,
Filled with good and glory,
How tenderly You swell my heart with love![9]

Mystics may speak in mystical hyperbole or apparent contradictions, trying to express what cannot be expressed in words and rational thought. I recall the *Four Quartets* of T. S. Eliot, whose mystical insights are filled with apparent contradictions:

In order to possess what you do not possess,
You must go by the way of dispossession,
In order to arrive at what you are not
You must go through the way in which you are not.
And what you do not know is the only thing you
    know
And what you own is what you do not own
And where you are is where you are not.[10]

T. S. Eliot's poem speaks the truth, but it is a mystical truth that the unaided intellect cannot grasp. Such intellectual contradictions, which occur often in mystical writings, are also doorways to the Truth. These contradictions silence the mind, and offer keys to tasting a deeper truth.

When the mystical door opens, God is calling the soul to learn through a spiritual "tasting" of the divine presence. Silence, poetry, song, symbol, and mystical hyperbole are all common ways mystics have tried to express this explosion of love and goodness in their hearts.

Once the door is opened, there is a lifetime of merely *beginning* to plumb the inexhaustible depths of God. The more one dives into the ocean of God, the more of the divine that opens up, the less one knows, and the "farther away" from God one feels.

In the end, mystics become the simplest of souls and they see themselves as the most inept of beginners. We all must humbly recognize that we are beginners. We listen and learn from others. When we try to share our spiritual insights, we do so as peers and ones hardly worthy to speak of such wonderful things, and the words we use do not do justice to a Truth that transcends the grasp of our human capacity.

After many years on the mystical journey, mystics learn to become beginners again. The inexhaustible being of God has become so overwhelming as to dwarf the few, little insights that we have. The blazing holiness of God makes our own little light seem insignificant. And the boundless goodness of God is unspeakable as to bring our hearts to awe and silence.

But if it is truly God whom we have tasted, this nothingness of ours brings us peace. The infinite majesty of God brings us to praise. And the goodness of God brings us joy.

We speak haltingly of a knowledge that can only be tasted and we wonder at the infinite riches that lie ahead. We are, now and ever more, the beginners. This is the mystical way.

I am always learning —

four

Friends

of God

HAVING BEEN TOUCHED BY THE BEGINNING GRACES OF GOD, individuals choose whether or not to accept God's invitation. Jesus predicted that all of the seed sown would not produce fruit, only those seeds that fell on good soil. There will be many other seeds that will fall on rocky soil, on the footpath, or among the thorns (Mt 13:1-9). This is a great sorrow: the many souls who do not respond to God's invitation.

However, those of generous heart, who desire to follow the Lord more closely, will answer the call. They will likely ask: "What should I do?" Being of good will and eager to please the Lord, we want to do the right thing. Of course, the answer to such a question is very personal and lies in a lifelong discernment of God's call for the individual.

However, for Christian mystics, the first question should not be, "What do I do?" but rather, "How should I be?" The mystical journey is preeminently a life that focuses on *being*, rather than doing. Mystics can be found in almost every walk of life and in every life circumstance and thus are largely indistinguishable in what they do. Rather, the sign of true mystics is in who they are. By God's grace, and through their acceptance of this grace, *they are friends of God*. As the mystic Teresa of Avila said, "For with His own mouth He praises them and considers them His friends."[11]

The very concept of being a friend of God is over-whelming. One might wonder if it is even appropriate to use such a word as "friend" when describing our rela tionship with God. After all, God is the all-powerful Creator and we are merely lowly creatures. Catherine of Siena relayed God's words to her, "I am he who is, and thou art that which is not."[12] But a true friendship can only be fostered between peers and there must be some equality in the relationship. How can the Creator and creature be friends?

The answer lies in the person of Jesus. Jesus is both divine and human. Thus, he is the portal and bridge to God. Jesus gave us the clear invitation to a friendship with himself, and thus a friendship with God. He declared,

I no longer call you slaves, because a slave does not know what his master is doing. I have called you friends, because I have told you everything I have heard from my Father. It was not you who chose me, but I who chose you. . . . (Jn 15:15-16)

We read in Jesus' words that he chooses us to be friends of God. We are not God's equals. Yet, God condescends to a true friendship with us that is only pos-sible because of the person of Jesus. Jesus is God's condescension toward humankind. He has made the impossible possible.

We are truly friends of God. This is a source of much joy. What joy to be a friend of God! In this friendship there is a delightful familiarity with God. We are beloved of God and he delights in hearing our voice. God himself finds joy in us. He, in turn, is the source of our joy. It is our greatest treasure simply to look upon the divine face and to gaze into his heart. Friends of God! We are truly such because he has invited us to be so.

To be a friend of God is a wonderful gift. We delight in his presence. We give thanks to him, not so much for what he does for us, but just because of who God is. We thank God for being God. We rejoice not in what a friend does for us, but simply for being a beautiful friend. And God rejoices, not in what we do for him, but simply because we are his friends. As it says in the Song of Songs, an Old Testament book often the favorite of mystics:

Ah, you are beautiful, my beloved,
ah, you are beautiful; your eyes are doves! (Sg 1:15)

How does this friendship with God manifest itself? The scriptural image of the intimacy that Adam and Eve enjoyed with God in the garden may be helpful. The Book of Genesis relates to us, "The man and his wife were both naked, yet they felt no shame" (Gn 2:25). In their close friendship with God, Adam and Eve were literally naked before God and each other. Theirs was a true intimacy and one not tainted by the debilitating effects of sin.

Because of our redemption in Christ, we, too, are called to such an intimacy with God. We can appear before him spiritually and emotionally naked. Rather than hiding ourselves from God, as Adam and Eve did after they had sinned, mystics learn to reveal themselves to God. All friendship includes some degree of self-revelation or the friendship cannot grow. *God continues to reveal himself to us; he calls us friends. We must learn to do the same.*

This step may be difficult, if not almost prohibitive, for some. We are all tainted by the residual effects of sin and thus we hide from God, from others, and from ourselves. Some find self-awareness particularly difficult and painful. But if we are to nourish a friendship with God, we must take the difficult path of learning about ourselves and facing the truth squarely. If we cannot face ourselves, we cannot face God. And we cannot share with God what we refuse to look at in ourselves. We must do so if our friendship with God is to grow.

Not long ago, I was working with a man dying of AIDS. I asked him how his prayer life was. He commented that he had stopped praying several months ago. When I asked him why, he told me that he prayed and prayed and prayed, but nothing happened. So he gave up. I asked him how he prayed and he said that he would go into the chapel and spend his time giving thanks and praise to God, but nothing happened. When I asked him how he really felt toward God, he said that he was frightened and angry at God. I suggested that he go back into the chapel and be honest with God. "Tell God exactly how you feel," I said, "Besides, if you and I both know you are angry at God, I am sure that he already knows." The man went back into the chapel, got angry at God, and his prayer life began to come alive again. He recently died a holy death.

I am reminded of the prayer of Moses, a real friend of God who the scriptures tell us spoke to God "face to face." At one point, Moses, in a fit of frustration, said to God, "If this is the way you will deal with me, then please do me the favor of killing me at once" (Nm 11:15). Similarly, Teresa of Avila, in a fit of pique, spoke her oft-quoted words to God, "If this is how you treat your friends, it's no wonder you have so few." Teresa, called the "Doctor of Prayer," taught us that prayer is "nothing but friendly intercourse, and frequent solitary converse, with Him," that is, prayer is a conversation between friends.[13]

Friendship requires honesty. We must be honest with God. Many times this means praying from our anger and our pain. What could be a more trusting prayer and a more helpful aid to our friendship with God than sharing with him the hurts, pains, and angers that lie in the center of our hearts? There is a time to praise and thank God in our prayer. There is also a time to trust him with the hurts that trouble us so much—even if we are angry at him.

God is truly our friend, who wants to share in our burdens. Mystics must learn to trust God and to give him a chance to help us. However, we must expose our real weaknesses and our most secret hurts and fears. We must become naked in front of God. This is one of the most difficult hurdles of the mystical path. Time and again the painful truths about ourselves beg to be faced and shared with God in prayer. Each moment represents an opportunity to dig deeper into the truth and thus move more deeply into our friendship with God. As Jesus said, "I am the Truth." As we move more deeply into the truth about ourselves, we move more deeply into Jesus who is the Truth.

Eventually, the mystical path takes us into a relaxed intimacy with God. As his friends, we enjoy a respectful familiarity just as Adam and Eve enjoyed in the garden. They knew the "sound of the Lord God moving in the garden at the breezy time of the day" (Gn 3:8). Like Adam and Eve, we come to recognize the "sound of the Lord" and, instead of hiding, we increasingly appear before the Lord naked and without shame. Teresa of Avila tells us, "It is a great thing to have experienced the friendship and favor He shows toward those who journey on this road."[14]

Mystics are friends of God. More than any supernatural revelation or mystical grace, the treasure of every mystic is God himself. He has reached down from the heavens and now walks with us on the earth. Our greatest gift and our everlasting joy is our friendship with God.

five

Facing Sin

Is Freedom

READING THE WORKS OF THE GREAT MYSTICS, ONE IS STRUCK BY their awareness of their own sinfulness. In fact, some of them seem almost obsessed with their sinfulness. Paragraph after paragraph, the mystics speak of their littleness, their brokenness, their weaknesses, and their sins. Oddly enough, they do not seem depressed by it. Their words have a ring of freedom, even joy. One might attribute some of this obsession with human sinfulness to the spirituality of past centuries. Many of these great mystics wrote in an era in which pronouncing one's sinfulness was *de rigeur*, that is, their writings followed the spiritual style of the times.

But the great mystics were not afraid to shock the sensibilities of the people of their times. If there is any group of writers who spoke the truth as they saw it, without much concern about how they would be received, it was the mystics. Their writings carry a compelling note of authenticity that echoes the truth down through the ages. Their insights are timeless.

Why then do the great mystics speak so often of their sinfulness? The answer is clear. *They speak so often of their sinfulness because it is the truth.* The truth is that, like them, we too are weak, broken, and small. Mystics have an acute awareness of this truth. Their awareness of this personal darkness is acute because they see the light. As the scriptures tell us, "If we say, 'We are without sin,' we deceive ourselves, and the truth is not in us" (1 Jn 1:8).

Ironically, and most dangerously, individuals ensnared in their sinfulness usually have little sense of their perilous situation. One of the most pernicious effects of sin is that sin carries with it a kind of blindness. The more we sin, the less we become aware of the darkness into which we are falling. As souls become less and less accustomed to goodness and the light of God, they find themselves blinded and forgetful of true joy and bliss. Eventually, they become like the Gerasene demoniac who lived amid the tombs and wandered day and night screaming and gashing himself with stones (Mk 5:1-20). The more we sin, the more we defile our true humanity and become like tortured animals. It is not difficult to see the many signs of this tortured state in the violence and rage in our society today; even now, we see so much of the darkness of hell.

On the other hand, the light of God illumines every inch of our beings and it shows us the truth. The light of God is glorious, but it is also painful. When the pure light of God shines on us, we are raised up in joy. We understand for the first time what true beauty and goodness are. We also understand, for the first time, the truth about sin and evil. It is for no small reason that Jesus includes in his great teaching on prayer the phrase, "Deliver us from evil." He wants us to pray this prayer often, "Deliver us from evil." Those who live in the light are justly and appropriately frightened of falling into the darkness.

Mystics who have begun to live in the light become painfully aware of their own sin and darkness. It is the light that shows how riddled we are with the flaws of darkness. *This is another hurdle of the mystical path: being willing to face within us the darkness and sin that lies there.* Some balk at this truth and turn back. It takes courage to face our own sinfulness. Those willing to undergo this painful enlightenment look with sadness at just how much sin and weakness lie within us. So, when the light comes, we see the darkness, too, and thus we begin the long journey toward healing and wholeness. *On into eternity*

In the fourth century, hermits lived in the deserts around Egypt and Palestine. They were great ascetics, deeply spiritual men and women, and were often referred to as the "Desert Fathers." Here is one of the many wonderful stories from their tradition:

> A brother in Scete happened to commit a fault, and the elders assembled, and sent for Abbot Moses to join them. He, however, did not want to come. The priest sent him a message, saying: Come, the community of the brethren is waiting for you. So he arose and started off. And taking with him a very old basket full of holes, he filled it with sand and carried it behind him. The elders came out to meet him, and said: What is this, Father? The elder replied: My sins are running out behind me, and I do not see them, and today I come to judge the sins of another! They, hearing this, said nothing to the brother but pardoned him.[15]

As friends of God, we have a special awareness and abhorrence of sin. We are anxious to do nothing that would hurt our friendship with God. While God is all-merciful, sin damages our friendship with God. Sin does not hurt God. Rather, sin damages us and obscures our true and blessed humanity that is made in the image of God. Mystics strive to flee from all sin.

Some mystics have spoken of the foul stench of evil. In the presence of the demonic, they have been repulsed by the terrible odor of sin and evil. When we do not see the beauty of goodness and God, we are not fully aware of the tragedy of sin. *We must not underestimate the damage of sin.* This is a danger of our time. If the previous error was to overemphasize our sinfulness, our era underestimates the reality and horror of evil and sin.

Those who accept the friendship of God should do everything possible to cease any and all serious sin. It is folly to think that we can continue to abuse our humanity, which is the result of all sin, and at the same time move closer to God. *The Cloud of Unknowing*, a great mystical text, teaches us, "If you ask me when a person should begin the contemplative work I would answer: not until he has first purified his conscience of all particular sins. . . ."[16] Those who are mired in serious sin must eventually turn away from such behaviors. It is true that God can, and does, touch individuals with his special graces even while they are ensnared in serious sin. However, the friends of God must eventually let go of such self-destructive behaviors and follow their Friend.

As we slowly put serious sin behind us, and it is likely to be a process of fits and starts for many, we increasingly wake up to the light. As the light shines in every crevasse of our being, we become increasingly aware of our sinfulness. While serious sin will hopefully become a thing of the past, the sinful condition and the utter human weakness that is ours becomes painfully obvious.

The closer one moves toward God, the stronger the pure light of God becomes. It pierces ever more clearly into our hearts, and thus we see ever more clearly the darkness that lies hidden within us. This is why the greatest mystics spoke often and strongly about their own sinfulness. They were not exaggerating the truth; it was not a kind of false humility. Rather, they spoke the real truth because they saw it clearly: our humanity is full of sin like a basket full of holes leaking out sand.

Paradoxically, as we move closer to God, we feel farther away from him. A true and irrefutable sign of real sanctity is an increasing, yet hope-filled, awareness of one's sinfulness. Despondent neurotics know their sinfulness, but are mired in this muck. Their awareness of sin does not spring from, nor lead to, the shining light of God. Without seeing one's sins in the light of God, we easily slide into despair. Perhaps this is why so many struggle against and avoid facing the truth of human sin.

Mystics, on the other hand, increasingly know their sinfulness in the light of God's goodness. Ironically this awareness of their sin makes them less weighed down by their fallen humanity. To know one's sinfulness in the light of God's forgiveness allows the soul to let go of one's sinful burden and to be lifted up in and into God. To know one's sinfulness in God's light is a grace. This grace is more sure and more effective than any ecstasy or special revelation. This is a grace to pray for: to know one's sinfulness!

Whether we are aware of it or not, sin weighs us down. Becoming aware of our own sinfulness in the light of God is a source of freedom. In this light we come ever more readily and thankfully to commend ourselves to the all-encompassing mercy of God. This is why the mystics' obsession with their own sinfulness seems almost joyful. They know that there is no sin so great that God cannot forgive. As great is our horror of sin, even greater is our rejoicing in the mercy of God.

six

Judge Not

HAVING BEEN INVITED TO BE FRIENDS OF GOD, WE GIVE THANKS and labor mightily not to soil so great a gift through serious sin. This is the most rudimentary of beginnings, but it is indispensable.

But after having given up serious sin, the soul is moved by grace to seek "more." The person is likely to have no real awareness of what this "more" is, but simply has some awareness that there is more available. The soul has an inner desire; it wants something although it is not quite sure what that something is. This stirring in the soul is the movement of grace.

This desire for "more" might remind us of the rich young man who came to Jesus. He had followed the commandments all his life but it was not enough. He refrained from serious sin but had an inkling that there was more being offered to him. Jesus confirmed his desire and told him that, indeed, there was more. Jesus extended to him an invitation: "Come, follow me" (Mt 19:21).

Similarly, there is a story from the Desert Fathers that is much the same:

> Abbot Lot came to Abbot Joseph and said: Father, according as I am able, I keep my little rule, and my little fast, my prayer, meditation and contemplative silence; and according as I am able I strive to cleanse my heart of thoughts; now what more should I do? The elder rose up in reply and stretched out his hands to heaven, and his fingers became like ten lamps of fire. He said: why not be totally changed into fire?[17]

Again, we see the story of someone who kept the external observance of the law. The law of the desert was prayer, meditation, silence, and cleansing of the heart. Abbot Lot kept the law of the desert, but it was not enough for him. He wanted more, and Abbott Joseph said indeed there was more. He offered, "Why not be totally changed into fire?"

Instinctively we recognize that our spiritual search cannot be satisfied in merely refraining from sin. Woe to any religion that only offers to its followers a moral code of do's and don'ts. Our hearts want, and demand, more. We have an inner urge that impels our souls into the unknown. *It is the mystic who has learned to feel this urge and to follow it.*

After having refrained from serious sin, mystics are ready to begin the long process of traveling into the unknown. With only an inner urge to guide them, mystics then must learn to let go of the rational supports of the past and begin to walk as blind beggars pushing their canes in front of them.

In the beginning we are truly blind. The kingdom of God is around us and in us. God's presence is everywhere. But we are blind. As Jesus told them, "If you were blind, you would have no sin; but now you are saying

'We see,' so your sin remains" (Jn 9:41). We are blinded by our sins, we are blinded by our five physical senses, and we are definitely blinded by the rational control we try to exert over everything. And the problem is that we do not even know that we are blind. Jesus challenged them, "Are your hearts hardened? Do you have eyes and not see, ears and not hear?" (Mk 8:17-18).

Our spiritual senses are blinded and clouded over by much "noise" and "dirt." One of the greatest sources of this spiritual "noise" is the judgments of our minds—our attempts to control everything. Thus, we are blinded by our pride, our desire to place ourselves in the position of a controlling God. These judgments of ours confound our inner peace and muddy our inner waters so that we cannot see clearly into the depths of our beings where God dwells. Nor can we see the kingdom of God that is everywhere around us.

After having given up serious sin, the next step is to move into the unknown in search of "something" of which we are only vaguely aware. We enter into the darkness as blind people, with only our trust that the small voice within us might possibly be the voice of God calling us. However, we cannot see much of anything and we certainly do not hear much of God's voice. So, we begin the slow process of learning to hear and see again; this time we learn to hear and see with the ears and eyes of our souls.

To do this, we must let go of our rational control and trust ourselves to God. The first step in this process of letting go of control is seemingly simple: *do not judge*. An early and essential step in the mystic journey is to stop judging others and, eventually, to stop judging one's self. This judging is our way of labeling, controlling, and demeaning. Instead, we must begin the process of trying to stop thinking and controlling everything. We must simply allow things to be.

The Desert Fathers tell a story that illuminates this truth:

A certain brother inquired of Abbot Pastor, saying: What shall I do? I lose my nerve when I am sitting alone at prayer in my cell. The elder said to him: Despise no one, condemn no one, rebuke no one, God will give you peace and your meditation will be undisturbed.[18]

To begin the mystical life in earnest, it is essential to stop judging others. Our intellectual judgments form a kind of barrier or screen to perceiving our inner selves and a barrier to perceiving the world. We do not "taste" the world because we separate ourselves from it with our rational judgments. As long as we hold onto our judgments, we hold onto our own rational control. Living a mystic life requires one to let go of control and to step into the darkness.

Jesus told us, "Stop judging and you will not be judged. Stop condemning and you will not be condemned" (Lk 6:37). He said this to us not primarily because of what it does to others, but because of what it does to us. Each time we judge others we separate ourselves from them. We wound our inner selves and we step back from really "touching" and "tasting" the truth. Ultimately, we step back from touching and tasting God.

When we stop judging, we silence our minds to the many noisy and arrogant thoughts we have about others. We have been setting ourselves up as judges and placing ourselves in a superior position. Ultimately, we have been trying to put ourselves in God's place. God alone is the one who has authority to judge.

Does this mean we accept everything uncritically? Of course we do not. Rather, the sins and failings of others do not cause us to rail in judgment. Because we have become aware of our own sinfulness that strikes us so forcefully and persistently, we find it difficult to condemn others. "Why do you notice the splinter in your brother's eye, but not perceive the wooden beam in your own?" (Lk 6:41).

Again, the Desert Fathers are instructive:

Abbot Joseph asked Abbot Pastor: Tell me how I can become a monk. The elder replied: If you want to have rest here in this life and also in the next, in every conflict with another say: Who am I? And judge no one.[19]

Ironically, I do not think that God really judges us either. Catherine of Genoa received a mystical insight that the gates of heaven are wide open. She said,

> As for paradise, God has placed no doors there.
> Whoever wishes to enter, does so.
> All-merciful God stands there with His arms open,
> Waiting to receive us into His glory.[20]

When people end up separated from God in a state we call "hell," I believe it is not because God has cast them off. Rather, it is because they have cast themselves off by walking away from God. *People are not thrust into hell by a judging God, rather they walk of their own accord into the "fires of perdition."* Theirs is the ultimate of follies. Their actions are complete madness. Yet, this is precisely what sin is: to commit the ultimate of follies by rejecting God and choosing hell.

When we stop judging, we begin the process of silencing the "noise" of our minds and the control they try to exert over God's creation. An inner peace begins to grow in us. We become more like our God who, although fully aware of our sinfulness and at times utter depravity, constantly extends to us his goodness and love. Should we strive to do any less, we who are full of sin?

Therefore, if we desire to know freedom from our own judgments and from the control and arrogance of our minds, judge not! It is a simple prescription but a most difficult challenge. It is much more difficult than refraining from serious sin and it takes much longer to attain. It may take a lifetime or more.

It is well for us to meditate more fully on the words of Jesus:

Stop judging and you will not be judged. Stop condemning and you will not be condemned. Forgive and you will be forgiven. Give and gifts will be given to you: a good measure, packed together, shaken down, and overflowing, will be poured into your lap. For the measure with which you measure will in return be measured out to you. (Lk 6:37-38)

This is the reward that awaits those who can stop judging and learn to forgive: "gifts will be given to you" in great abundance. These gifts will be so plentiful that they will be poured into our spiritual laps until they overflow. Judging and parsimonious thinking cause us to be stingy and eventually our spirit dries up in a nasty scowl.

God, on the other hand, invites us to be like himself. God does not judge, but gives freely and generously to all. Our God "makes his sun rise on the bad and the good, and causes rain to fall on the just and the unjust" (Mt 5:45). This does not seem fair: why should God be good to those who are bad? But the truth is that the offer of God's boundless love is made to everyone at every moment, even to sinners like us. As Paul the Apostle told us, "But God proves his love for us in that while we were still sinners Christ died for us" (Rom 5:8).

God gives to all with a boundless generosity. As we stop judging, we let go of our pride-filled control. As we stop judging, we make room in our hearts and minds for God to pour in limitless gifts. As we stop judging, we become like God who showers his love on the bad and the good alike.

Then God's presence becomes more fully alive in our hearts. The inner noise softens and we become aware of a gentle inner light. We begin to hear the sound of God's goodness. We look out at the world and notice a gentle radiance. God was here all along, smiling his beautiful smile at us. Only now do we begin to see and hear him. What joy it is finally to see and hear our Friend.

seven

The Need

to Be Guided

NAVIGATING THE MYSTICAL JOURNEY CAN BE A BIT OF A minefield. The story of a monk named Hero, as related by John Cassian, is a chilling reminder. Hero was an exemplary monk and ascetical hermit of the desert for fifty years. But he was deluded by an angel of Satan into thinking that the merit of his virtue and his many years of rigorous self-denial would protect him from harm. Thus, he was tempted to throw himself down a dark well believing that he would be miraculously protected. Sadly, he plunged into the well and was subsequently pulled out of the well by another brother. Hero died from his injuries two days later. As he lay dying, Hero still would not give up his delusion and recognize that he had erred.[21]

While this story is an extreme example, the dangers of self-delusion, whether being misled by the evil one or simply exercising bad judgment, are very real. I have seen some people, in the wake of what appeared to be a genuine mystical experience, all but destroy their family in the belief that they were called to a "special" life, away from their worldly responsibilities. Several others have fallen into a kind of "quietism" in which their meditations only served to dampen their emotional lives, not enliven them. Others have understood their mystical graces as a sign that they were called out of their communities of faith to follow a solitary, unique journey. However, the path they chose did not take them into true solitude, but left them without community support, emotionally isolated, and at a spiritual dead end.

The frightening part of all these stories is that the individuals who made these decisions did so in "good faith," that is, they honestly believed that the path they were choosing was the right one. And they followed this path at considerable personal sacrifice. Nevertheless, all indications would suggest that they were badly mistaken. "By their fruits you will know them" (Mt 7:20). The common factor in all of these stories is that all the individuals involved directed their own spiritual lives. They followed their own designs.

The errors made by mystics, whether in good faith or not, are no less possible or devastating than the errors that people have been making for centuries, and continue to make, in the name of religion. People continue to kill each other in the name of God; they torture and enslave others, and force "conversions." In more "civilized" nations, people are verbally judged, condemned, and executed without a drop of blood. *No one is more dangerous than a religious zealot.*

There is no simple way to ensure that wrong decisions will not be made. There is no sure-fire method or technique to make sure that the right path will be taken. In fact, one can be assured of making some mistakes along the way. I suspect that most of us who look back on our earliest spiritual days will grimace at many of our early attitudes and decisions. Indeed, this ability to look back and see how one has erred and changed is a sign of spiritual growth. Hopefully the mistakes we make will not be major or life-threatening. But there are ways to minimize mistakes and to assist one's growth in the mystical life.

One of these ways is spiritual direction. At any time in the spiritual journey, enlisting the aid of a spiritual guide can be helpful. However, in the beginning and during times of particular difficulty and/or discernment, spiritual direction is essential. "Behind every saint stands another saint. That is the great tradition. I never learnt anything myself by my own old nose."[22] We are largely unaware of our weaknesses and we are easily led astray by self-deception. The presence of an experienced spiritual guide can be a life-saving grace, as well as a real consolation.

Neophytes in the mystical journey may be reticent to consult a spiritual director. As the anonymous author of *The Cloud of Unknowing* wrote, "I must warn you that a young novice, unseasoned by experience in contemplation, is liable to great deception unless he is constantly alert and honest enough to seek reliable guidance."[23] First of all, their own hubris can delude them into thinking that they do not need a director but can follow the Spirit's guidance on their own. They also may look about and believe that there is no one who is "up to the task." This, too, is spiritual narcissism.

Neophyte mystics may be reluctant to speak about their spiritual experiences, and rightly so. Communications between God and an individual soul are highly personal and intimate. They should be treated just as privately as the intimate secrets of a married couple. In addition, it is hard to verbalize one's spiritual experiences and neophytes are likely to fear that they will, at best, not be believed, or at worst, be ridiculed. The reticence to speak of one's intimate spiritual experiences is a healthy one. Nevertheless, a wise spiritual guide should be made privy to everything. Without complete honesty, especially regarding one's intimate relationship with God, there is little benefit to be gained.

It is true that authentic spiritual guides are hard to find, and there is no central registry or licensing process for spiritual directors. How can one be assured that an individual speaks the truth? After all, not all guides are good ones. As the scriptures tell us, "If a blind person leads a blind person, both will fall into a pit" (Mt 15:14).

If a good spiritual guide can be found, I heartily recommend spiritual direction. Such a guide will be a wise person who will be a sounding board, offering insights and encouragement for the journey. Sometimes the relationship will be deeper and the spiritual director will be a kind of mentor and companion, accompanying the directee on the journey. Then there are those rare experiences in which the spiritual director will be a direct conduit of grace for the learner: a spiritual parent. Thomas Merton spoke of this unique relationship:

> It must not be forgotten that the spiritual director in primitive times was much more than the present name implies. He was a spiritual father who "begot" the perfect life in the soul of his disciple by his instructions first of all, but also by his prayer, his sanctity and his example. He was to the young monk a kind of "sacrament" of the Lord's presence in the ecclesiastical community.[24]

This intimate spiritual parenting is evidenced in the prophets Elisha and his spiritual father Elijah. Toward the end of Elijah's life, Elisha asked, "May I receive a double portion of your spirit" (2 Kgs 2:9), that is, Elisha asked to be treated as Elijah's first-born son who inherited a double portion of his father's property. Indeed, Elisha did succeed Elijah as Israel's prophet. When Elijah left this earth, his spirit came to Elisha who took up his master's mantle in his place. The spiritual father imparted to his spiritual offspring the grace that he himself had received.

The mystical journey, like life itself, is fraught with many blind alleys and real dangers. More than a few have seriously strayed off the path, to their own peril. A spiritual guide can be a great help and a blessing. I hope that God graces each seeker with one. If not, God will send a "teacher" of a different sort. The spiritual classic *The Way of the Pilgrim* teaches us in this regard:

> In the practice of the interior activity of the heart it is necessary to have an experienced spiritual director. . . . If, however, you cannot find one, with a humble and contrite heart call on God to help you to apply the precepts and direction of the teachings of the Fathers and to verify this with the word of God as given in Holy Scripture. In this regard, it is also important to keep in mind he who is sincere in his spiritual search will recognize true instruction even when it comes from simple, ordinary people.[25]

Most people are not blessed with a spiritual director. Therefore, there are a number of other "teachers" that one can use to keep on the narrow path. Books on the mystical journey are a source of instruction and they are almost always used extensively by other mystics. God can and does inspire us while reading the works of the great ones. Teresa of Avila, the Desert Fathers, Therese of Lisieux, Brother Lawrence, the mystical doctor himself—John of the Cross—and many others have all trod the path before us and have left guideposts for us in their writings. We should have regular recourse to their insights (a select bibliography is provided at the back of this book). In the beginning, if we do not understand the insights of the great masters, spiritual maturity will help us eventually to understand them. The divine Guide puts the right books in our hands when the time has come. It is through the printed word that we come in contact with much of the great mystical wisdom that has been handed down through the centuries.

And, of course, the greatest book to guide us is the living word of God. The sacred scriptures not only guide us infallibly toward the Father, this word carries within it the living Spirit of God. Thus, the word of God is our surest guide and is itself a boundless source of grace.

The mystical life carries with it a special source of guidance and inspiration. Integral to this life is a direct and consistent contact with God. Not only is this communication between God and mystics ongoing, it results in an ever-deepening communion of hearts and wills. The scriptures confirm this: "As for you, the anointing that you received from him remains in you, so that you do not need anyone to teach you. But his anointing teaches you about everything and is true and not false; just as it taught you, remain in him" (1 Jn 2:27).

As mystics ever more deeply "remain in him," their beings are increasingly in harmony with God. Thus, God assists in directly guiding the mystics. However, the disastrous end of the monk Hero should serve as a warning. We do not always discern rightly the will of God, thus the scriptural admonition, "Beloved, do not trust every spirit but test the spirits to see whether they belong to God" (1 Jn 4:1).

Ultimately, we use a combination of all these "teachers" at different moments in our lives. We stay close to the scriptures, meditating upon them often. We regularly read the writings of the great mystics and take in their wisdom. From time to time we are fortunate to have a spiritual director to guide us. Perhaps once in our lives we are blessed to have a spiritual parent who shares grace directly with us. We listen to the everyday wisdom of those around us. And always, we stay attuned to the God who dwells within. We rejoice to hear the voice of our Friend and follow him willingly.

Regardless of how God leads at each moment, be assured that we do need assistance. Any other thought is sheer arrogance and it is arrogance that leads one astray.

eight

Living for
God Alone

AN ESSENTIAL FEATURE OF THE MYSTICAL PATH IS MAKING THE decision to live for God alone. The end of the mystical path is a complete and total union with God. He does not accept an adulterous heart and there can be no one or no thing in his place. "I, the LORD, am your God. . . .You shall not carve idols for yourselves. . . . I, the LORD, your God, am a jealous God" (Ex 20:2, 4, 5).

However, this decision takes a lifetime to make real. In the beginning, we consciously choose to live for God alone, but our hearts are torn in many directions. We are beset by the idols of lust, avarice, spiritual weakness, pride, tepidity, and many other vices. We are filled with many "normal" human weaknesses. We want to be liked and approved by others. We want to be held in high esteem. We want to be in positions of power and exercise authority. Thus, our hearts are wedded to many other things besides God. It takes a lifetime to learn to live for God alone.

Living for God alone does not necessarily mean leaving one's family or place of business. While time away from the distractions of the world can be a great help in fostering this relationship with God, especially in the beginning, mystics will have to find the place and modality in which they are called to find the Lord.

Some great mystics have led very busy lives. Others have been buried in desert solitudes. Some have reared large families and ruled nations, while others have led a hidden, unknown life. Therese of Lisieux scrubbed floors giving us the "Little Way" while John Vianney spent long hours listening to other people's sins in the confessional.

It matters little which vocational path is chosen so long as it is the right one for the individual and thus blessed by God. Remember, grace is freely given as a gift. Choosing an ascetical vocation or an overtly "religious" vocation will not be helpful if it is not in harmony with God's will. "Obedience is better than sacrifice, and submission than the fat of rams" (1 Sm 15:22). We recall the primary rule of the mystical life: all is gift and grace. *The mystical journey is not a reward for an ascetical life.*

But, the key is, in whatever path one is called, to enter it with a full heart and to live as completely as one can for God. We cannot enter the mystical path thinking that it will be a hobby or something to do in our spare time. It must become a life-changing and all-embracing totality. There will be trials and tests along the way. If we cling to anything except God, we will not finish the journey. "No one who sets a hand to the plow and looks to what was left behind is fit for the kingdom of God" (Lk 9:62). Once again, it is important to note that this full conversion to God will take a lifetime. God calls very imperfect people to follow his intimate way.

There is a spiritual practice that can foster and enhance one's total conversion and self-gift to God. The scriptures admonish us, "Let us rid ourselves of every burden and sin that clings to us . . . while keeping our eyes fixed on Jesus" (Heb 12:1-2). Indeed, many great mystics have used this expression, "Fixing one's eyes on God" or "Focusing one's eye on Christ." This is not simply a metaphor. It speaks of a deep truth in the mystical life. This was a grace Brother Lawrence of the Resurrection, another spiritual teacher, had himself received. He related, "What comforts me in the life is that I see God by faith in such a manner that I can sometimes say: 'I no longer believe, but I see.'"[26]

The more one's inner spirit becomes attuned to God and focuses on him, the more one "sees" God. The mystic learns, by grace, to see God constantly. This is a great source of joy and consolation. While this vision is, of course, not the consummation of the beatific vision that will only be possible in the next life, it is a real "inchoate" vision of God. The inner spirit senses the presence of God and focuses one's spiritual eye on him.

As we learn this inner way of focusing our eyes on God, we learn how to walk more confidently in the mystical path. Our steps become stronger and we feel more assured of our way. Fear is more and more banished and we begin to run toward the final goal.

This focusing our eyes on God is a wonderful grace and it enlivens the soul. Mystics feel the presence of the Beloved and turn their spiritual gaze toward him. As Augustine shared in his autobiographical and mystical work, *Confessions*:

On entering into myself I saw, as it were with the eye of the soul, what was beyond the eye of the soul, beyond my spirit: your immutable Light.[27]

The immutable light of God's presence then overshadows everything and, at the same time, enlivens everything. This presence of God gives meaning to everything for the mystic. Thus, ironically, the mystic actually gives up nothing in living for God alone and gains everything.

One night, a sacristan saw Thomas Aquinas kneeling in ecstasy before the church cross. A voice, which seemed to come from the cross, said aloud, "Thou hast written well of me, Thomas; what reward wouldst thou have?" Thomas answered, "Nothing but Thee."[28] As the greatest of theologians, Thomas knew that to have God is to have everything. To decide to give up all for God actually results in our giving up very little and gaining everything. Like the person who found a buried treasure in a field; he gave up everything he had and bought the field (Mt 13:44-46). And he got a great deal!

This grace of being able to focus one's eyes on God may be given farther down the mystical path and is not usually given to the beginner. This grace brings to life the admonition of the scriptures to keep "our eyes fixed on Jesus." When this grace is given, it seems easier to live for God alone since his presence comes into the "field of vision" of the mystic. As we gaze upon God, we realize that he is all things and the source of all goodness and blessing. We come to know that all is "straw" compared to the beauty and goodness of our God. Our hearts become entranced with God and surge up in joy. At this moment, we are focused completely on God.

And then we fall back to earth. We realize that this moment of absorption in God has been a grace. In the beginning, we can only live for God alone for a few moments, then we fall back into human weakness. We are necessarily taken up with our worldly cares and duties. But, slowly, we begin the process again, searching for him again, waiting upon his grace, and focusing our inner eye on our God.

Eventually, mystics integrate their inner focus on God and their lives in the world. Whether they are surrounded by children or walled up in a hermitage, mature mystics bring together within themselves simultaneously a consciousness of the divine and the enfleshment of a full humanity. This unity mirrors the incarnation of Jesus who is both God and fully human. Thus, mystics are simultaneously at peace in the world and their hearts are filled with the delight of God.

The mystic must live for God alone, searching, waiting, focusing, praying. This total focus demands sacrifice and discipline. But, in the end, we recognize that coming to the moment of living for God alone is itself a grace. It is a grace that is generously given and a profound blessing. It is then that we are at peace with the world around us and, at the same time, we gaze with delight upon the beauty of our Beloved's face.

Pray for the grace of living for God alone. Having received it, one is given all things besides.

nine

Thy Will

Be Done

IN THE INITIAL FERVOR OF ENTERING THE MYSTICAL PATH, THE
neophyte is likely to embrace willingly ascetical practices.
This is a good impulse. Every true form of mysticism,
Christian and otherwise, includes an ascetical regimen.
Fasting, extended periods of prayer, abstinence from
worldly distractions, restraining one's sexual impulses,
and a variety of other deprivations of mind and body are
typically employed in the mystical way. Indulging one's
every desire and filling the mind with worldly matters
does *not* prepare the soul to receive the Spirit.

A life of discipline helps to rein in the passions and
aids in strengthening the spirit. As the years pass, we are
more able to receive the stronger yet subtler graces. I
believe that God gives us, at each moment, the greatest

and most abundant graces possible. However, if we are not ready for such graces, the strongest ones would lead us into spiritual pride and/or can be too much for our weak spirits. Too often we are able only to receive lesser graces. Ascetical practices help to strengthen and purify the spirit thus preparing it to receive God's stronger graces. Nevertheless, it should be said that God himself directly prepares the soul to receive him; our ascetical practices do a minimal, though important, amount of preparation.

A story from the Desert Fathers illustrates the need to purify the mind in order to gaze upon the divine: "One of the Fathers said: Just as it is impossible for a man to see his face in troubled water, so too the soul, unless it be cleansed of alien thoughts, cannot pray to God in contemplation."[29]

When engaging in ascetical practices, balance is needed. As noted previously, neophytes are often tempted to over-indulge in physical penances. They can be given to extremes during this early fervor. As it warns in *The Cloud of Unknowing*, "Neglecting the inspiration of grace and excited by vanity and conceit, he strains his endurance so morbidly that in no time he is weary and enervated in body and spirit."[30] In doing so they are unconsciously violating the primary rule: grace is a gift and cannot be earned. There is no amount of ascetical practice that can bring down the favor of God. While ascetical practices are necessary and important to curb one's unruly appetites and dispose one to the movements of the Spirit, they do not, of themselves, merit mystical favors. *The Cloud of Unknowing* concludes, "For the love of God, then, be careful and do not imprudently strain yourself in this work. Rely more on joyful enthusiasm than on sheer brute force."[31]

Nevertheless, the other extreme is also a delusion. It would be a mistake not to rein in one's desires and it is folly to eschew a life of discipline. There are many would-be gurus who promote self-indulgence and carnal excess.

Their way leads only to death. The mystical life is necessarily a disciplined life and if individuals cannot control their desires in a healthy way, there is little hope that they will progress beyond the earliest stages. A worse end is even possible: "The last condition of that person is worse than the first" (Lk 11:26).

Knowing how and when to discipline oneself requires a continual discernment and sensitivity to the movements of the Spirit. It also requires an increasing degree of self-knowledge and thus an awareness of one's weaknesses. After all, penances are not done for their own sake, but to curb the excesses of the self. A salutary discipline for one person might be a danger for another. Therefore, it is important for budding mystics to have a sense of the nature of their weaknesses and failings. Thus, one can apply the proper salve to the wound, that is, the proper penance to curb one's specific failings. The counsel of a spiritual director can be helpful.

Clearly, there are some basic disciplines that all spiritual people will want to adopt. Regarding physical penances, controlling one's appetites for food, drink, and sex will be essential. Curbing one's tongue and foregoing judgments about others have already been mentioned as essential psychological disciplines. A subtle spiritual discipline for the young mystic will be to curb one's appetite for spiritual consolations. Consolations are a wonderful gift from God but, if coveted for their own sake, they become an obstacle to seeking God in himself. God is more than consolations.

Initially, ascetical practices cause us some distress and discomfort. But toward the end of the journey they are less burdensome and become integrated into a spiritual life that gives us much joy and peace. The mature mystic comes to realize that what appeared in the beginning to be a penitential life was simply a balanced and wholesome life for any soul. In the beginning, however, filled with weakness and the effects of sin, this wholesome life is experienced as a sacrifice.

The first and most important penance of the mystical journey has nothing to do with what one eats or drinks, or with any of the carnal desires. "For the kingdom of God is not a matter of food and drink" (Rom 14:17). Rather, the first penance is *letting go of one's own will in favor of God's will*. There is no more important penitential prayer for mystics than the prayer Jesus taught us, "Thy will be done." Any other penance is subject to excesses and can easily lead to spiritual pride. All other penances have no intrinsic worth of themselves and can easily be counter-productive when done in the wrong spirit.

On the other hand, the first and most important penance is placing constantly on one's lips, "Thy will be done." Any act, whether seemingly laudatory or not, if not done in consonance with God's will, is useless. It is God who gives life and meaning to all things. The least gesture, when done in accordance with God's will, can itself be salvific. "Anyone who gives you a cup of water to drink because you belong to Christ, amen, I say to you, will surely not lose his reward" (Mk 9:41).

Mystics learn to attune their wills to the divine will. They learn to listen to God's will resonating in their hearts. As the scriptures tell us: "The wind blows where it wills, and you can hear the sound it makes, but you do not know where it comes from or where it goes; so it is with everyone who is born of the Spirit" (Jn 3:8). Mystics learn the "sound" of God by experience, a kind of con-naturality. We attune our spiritual ears, not primarily to our own needs, but first to God's will. We trust that following the divine will is the best for all, including ourselves.

If ascetical practices and long hours of prayer do any good at all, they help us to learn the sweet taste of God. Being expelled from the "garden," we have lost this familiarity with God and thus have been estranged from him. It is a long trek back to learn the taste of God and the sound of his voice. However, we have a sure guide. This sure guide is God's will.

We humans have only a little and faint desire to come home to God. Fortunately, God has an ever-burning and intense desire to bring us home to him. *God's will is a beacon in the spiritual night that constantly shines and leads us home.* Day in and day out, mystics strain to find the light of this beacon. Day in and day out, mystics strain to follow its light. They know that any other light will lead them to a spiritual shipwreck. The beacon of God's will is our only sure hope.

As we become more accustomed to finding this beacon and steady ourselves in following this light, we find our confidence in God rising and our Christian optimism growing. As we move closer and closer to the safe harbour of God, our desire to return home grows stronger. The little penances we performed in the past seem so small and fade from our consciousness, and we learn for ourselves the truth of Jesus' words, "For my yoke is easy, and my burden light" (Mt 11:30).

ten

Waiting

ANOTHER SALUTARY AND DIFFICULT ASCETICAL PRACTICE, AND paradoxically one of asceticism's increasing joys, is *waiting*. Mystics, as they move ever closer to God, find their hearts enlivened at the sound of his voice. They feel joy in contemplating God's goodness and delight in the radiance of his presence. It was said of Moses that "the skin of his face had become radiant while he conversed with the LORD" (Ex 34:29).

Yet, these moments of joy are fleeting. We cannot reach out and grab onto God. When we try to grab onto him, he remains always just beyond our fingertips. Only God can reach across the abyss and touch us. Only God can bestow the cool drops of divine grace on our tongues.

As mystics move closer and closer to God, their desire for him increases. In the beginning they are filled with much sin and many disordered desires. Their hearts are more attuned to these carnal desires and disordered pleasures. God is often far from their minds and they do not ardently search for him. Instead, they crave and indulge in worldly distractions. Even as the mystical door opens and the journey commences, beginners have only a little desire for God.

But as the soul matures, it comes to desire the "solid food" of God. It learns to value and long for an intimacy with God. He alone can satisfy the longings of our hearts. The more we taste him, the greater in turn our desire for him. *Thus, even the desire for God is a grace given by God.* As Augustine said in his autobiographical and mystical work, *Confessions*:

> You breathed your fragrance on me; I drew in breath and now I pant for you. I have tasted you, now I hunger and thirst for more. You touched me, and I burned for your peace.[32]

Therefore, as mystics move closer to God, their desire for him increases and yet, they must wait. They must wait on God. Only he can cross the abyss between divinity and humanity, between heaven and earth. Consolations are few and the periods of dryness are long. And so . . . we wait. We watch and we pray.

One might ask, "How do mystics pray?" The answer is clear: mystics pray by keeping watch. Their prayer is a vigil, ever alive to the presence of God. They increasingly learn to open their spiritual eyes to the sight of God. They learn to open their ears to the sound of his voice. Whether in a church, a hermitage, or a marketplace, mystics are always in prayer because they are constantly keeping vigil.

With the lamps of their souls alight, mystics hold constant vigil. They are vigilant souls. In keeping the vigil, they keep alive the communion between God and humankind. This is the great contribution and ministry of mystics: to be a bridge between the human and the divine. If there were not some who fulfilled this

Christlike role, it might be that the springs of divine grace
would not reach down so readily to the earth.

Ironically and indescribably, it is in the process of
becoming truly vigilant, of learning to be awake and
waiting, that mystics become fully alive to God's presence. It is not the consolations that ultimately speak to us
of God. No, it is *not* the consolations. Rather, it is, paradoxically, the waiting. As we learn to wait, we become
awake. In the very act of keeping vigil, we become awake
to God's presence. In fact, consolations themselves can be
a distraction to this true communion with God. We are
most alive in God when we are "awake" and keeping
vigil.

Waiting on the Lord and keeping constant vigil is the
role of mystics. It establishes the mystic bridge between
heaven and earth, between divinity and humanity. As
Christ is the bridge between God and humankind, mystics participate in Christ by themselves becoming, in
Christ, humanity filled with divinity.

This role of standing in the breach is a source of both
pain and sweetness for mystics. As John of the Cross says,
"O sweet cautery, O delightful wound!"[33] We are wound-
ed by the love of God and we feel the pain of our distance
from him. We long for him and desire him. Yet, this desire
is itself the prompting of grace. The desire is itself a sign of
God's Spirit working in the soul. Thus, there is a sweetness
in the pain, a sense of connectedness in the abandonment.

In this spiritual journey, sweetness and pain are often
intertwined. We must learn not to be too buoyed up by
the sweetness or too downcast by the pain. In fact, neither
state is any better than the other. They are both different
sides of the same experience of God. In the mystic journey, as in any Christian life, there is much sweetness and
much pain, and we learn to accept both with a sense of
peace.

Waiting is the joy of mystics and it is their penance. It
is a long, sometimes painful calling. But as we learn to
wait, we become alive to God who is always present.

When we keep vigil, we become like him who is ever vigilant, ever present. In fact, it is not that we keep vigil because we are actually "waiting for God." *No, the truth is that in becoming vigilant, we become like him who said, "I AM"* (Ex 3:14).

eleven

God Is

the Present

IT IS VERY TEMPTING TO LIVE IN THE PAST. IN FACT, MOST OF US
do. Psychologists tell us that most of our conscious
thoughts are thoughts of the past. We replay old scenes in
our minds; we fight old battles; we recall past joys; and
most of all we find ourselves stuck in the pains of the
past. We spend much energy reliving old scenes over and
over again. The sad part is that the past is over.

The second most common place for our minds to dwell,
after the past, is in the future. Our minds are filled with
hopes, fantasies, and fears for the future. We want to create
a future exactly as we dream it should be. We have an ideal
vision and want to realize that vision, but our fears and
conflicts nag at us, jeopardizing our future. Ironically,
most of our fears for the future never materialize. As Jesus

admonished us, "Do not worry about tomorrow; tomorrow will take care of itself. Sufficient for a day is its own evil" (Mt 6:34).

Like the shadows of the past, the visions of the future are not real. In themselves, neither has substance. Both the pains of our past and the fears of the future take up an enormous amount of our time and energy. We are prisoners of our own selves. These images in our minds currently do not exist, if they ever did. Most important, these images take us away from the place where all reality truly exists: the present. We have only the present. But we are rarely present to it. So, we squander our only reality, the present, on our useless fears and old hurts.

The mystical life is one that moves our consciousness out of the shadows of a gray, ephemeral existence that is the past and the future. It moves into a solid reality; it lives in the present. The mystical life is a real life. *One of the most important spiritual exercises for the mystic is to live in the present, that is, to live in reality.* Mystics become focused on the here and now; they face reality. However, this is not an easy task and we are rarely successful for long. Our minds easily slip into the past and race ahead to the future. Sadly, we find our fears and our old pains more comfortable than the blazing light of the Truth.

In moving to the past or future, the mind escapes from itself and the present, and thus escapes from what is True and Real. But as we begin to live in the present, we move out of the shadows of illusions and begin truly to face ourselves and to face God. This can be painful. Brother Lawrence confirmed this when he related that remaining in the presence of God is "a bit painful in the beginning."[34]

As noted previously, humans try very hard to escape facing their true selves and facing God. We unconsciously choose to live in the safe shadows of the past and the future. We are like people constantly tuned to an old movie on a television set whose images are not real. These images seem to be alive but they are only two-dimensional projections that engage and amuse the mind. When we step out of the "picture shows" of our minds into the present, we face the solid and three-dimensional truth.

In the *Republic*, Plato gives an apt analogy of life as if it were lived in a cave. He said, "Imagine human beings living in an underground, cave-like dwelling." Plato said that these individuals had always lived in the cave, chained and facing the cave wall. All that they saw and knew were the images that appeared on the cave wall. Behind them was reality as lived in the light, but they only saw the shadows. Plato noted, "Then the prisoners would in every way believe that the truth is nothing other than the shadows" of real life. He went on to say:

> And if someone compelled him to look at the light itself, wouldn't his eyes hurt, and wouldn't he turn around and flee towards the things he's able to see, believing that they're really clearer than the ones he's being shown? . . . And when he came into the light, with the sun filling his eyes, wouldn't he be unable to see a single one of the things now said to be true . . . he'd need time to get adjusted before he could see things in the world above.[35]

We are people who live in the shadows, accustomed to the darkness, and not even aware of the light.

Ironically, the more we live in the present, the more we are able to let go of useless fears and old hurts. When trapped in our fears of the future, they become exaggerated into little, and not too little, terrors. Similarly, most of our old hurts should have been let go a long time ago. It is only in the present that we find freedom from the tyranny of our fears and hurts.

Not surprisingly, in dodging the Truth and Reality, the mind becomes attached to its own false self and avoids falling into the hands of the living God. God is in our present. He is not in "heaven," if one describes heaven as some distant place in the future. He is not a God of history, if one describes history as being some distant place in the past. Rather, God calls himself "I am," and thus he is forever present to himself and to us. And when we are truly alive, it is because we are living in the present with and in God. The mystics' heaven is in God who is now.

It is commonly said that God is "eternal." However, if one defines "eternal" as being an endless amount of time, then it is misleading to call God "eternal." God does not live in time. It is more accurate to say that God is *beyond* time. Human beings live in time because they change. Time is a measure of change. God, on the other hand, lives in an infinite, changeless, dynamic present that is constantly unfolding and yet constantly remaining the same. God's changelessness is not static but dynamic. God does not live in our past or our future, but is standing right in front of us, right now, staring us in the face. But we constantly "look away" as we escape mostly into the past and sometimes into the future.

The truth is that God is in our present. The more our minds stay in the now, the more we are present to ourselves, to others and to God. The present is the gateway to God. Actually, God defined himself with the statement, "I AM" (Ex 3:14). Since reality is only in the present and God revealed to Catherine of Siena, "I am He who is," it may be more accurate to say starkly: *God is the timeless present.*

Mystics need go nowhere to find God. As T. S. Eliot, wrote, "Here and there does not matter, we must be still and still moving."[36] The more we are present to the Present, the more we live in God. The more we live in God, the more we enter into his timelessness.

One of the telltale signs of a true mystical experience is its timeless quality. Mystical experiences are nothing more than coming in direct contact with God. When we do so, we enter into God's reality. An important part of this reality is that God is beyond time. When we experience God, we lose a sense of time during the experience. This is the reason that mystics often cannot tell how long an experience of God lasted. It could have been just a moment or it could have lasted hours. T. S. Eliot captured this timeless quality in his mystical poem:

. . . at the still point, there the dance is,
But neither arrest nor movement. And do not call it
      fixity,
Where past and future are gathered. Neither
      movement from nor towards . . .
There would be no dance, and there is only the
      dance.
I can only say, *there* we have been: but I cannot say
      where.
And I cannot say, how long, for that is to place it in
      time.[37]

When the mystic "comes back to earth" there may be signs of how much time has elapsed such as the setting of the sun or the change in the time on a clock, but during the experience itself there is a lack of awareness of time.

This timelessness of God is supported by descriptions of the beatific vision. The blessed live in God. Thus, as it is with God, so it is with the blessed: "With the Lord one day is like a thousand years and a thousand years like one day" (2 Pt 3:8). The joy of true heaven, that is, the joy of being filled with God, will be experienced as a timeless and dynamic unfolding of God, and yet not a moment will pass. Time will be irrelevant.

Even in this life, mystics become increasingly filled with the timelessness of God. It may be, and it is most likely true, that mystics slowly find themselves less engaged in the passing of time. They increasingly find themselves living in a timeless present and gazing upon the One who is timeless. No longer victims of the past or paralyzed by the future, mystics live in the present and thus they live in God. And, like God and in God, they step out of the shadows and they become real.

twelve

Pray

Always

As the mystics travel farther down the path, their concept of prayer changes. In the beginning, prayer is something that humans do. We kneel down or perhaps we sit quietly and we begin to pray. We offer our thoughts and words to God. We make our petitions. Perhaps we even progress to the point where we regularly stop our petitioning and spend time listening to God in quiet meditation. This listening to God is an advanced and important form of prayer. These prayer forms are all good, but there is more. Such notions and forms of prayer are limited by an anthropomorphic concept of God, that is, an understanding of God that is bound by human constructs.

First of all, we must harken back to the basic principle of mysticism: the spiritual life is purely and totally a gift. Thus, any capacity we have to pray is a gift. Prayer itself is a gift. It is the Spirit of God in us that prays:

> The Spirit too comes to the aid of our weakness; for we do not know how to pray as we ought, but the Spirit itself intercedes with inexpressible groanings. (Rom 8:26)

Real prayer would never occur to us nor would it be possible without the movement of grace. Does it make a difference if we recognize that prayer is a gift? Absolutely. If we do not, we cannot move to mystical forms of prayer nor will we fulfill the scriptural injunction to "pray without ceasing" (1 Thes 5:17).

Indeed, the scriptures teach us to "pray always" (Lk 18:1). This is impossible if we think of prayer primarily as a human action that we initiate. As finite humans, we cannot attend to any action, such as prayer, twenty-four hours a day. More than a few people become discouraged when they read that they are to "pray always." It seems to be an impossible task or beyond their capacity, and they are correct.

However, if prayer is God's action working inside us, we can, and indeed we must, pray always. We need only open ourselves to the perpetual action of God in us who prays. Perpetual prayer becomes the heartfelt desire of mystics. It is their fervent desire to pray always because it is their one true wish to be perpetually and ever more deeply united with their beloved. Nothing makes sense or has any value unless it is wrapped in prayer, that is, wrapped in God's presence. God evokes in his mystics this desire for perpetual prayer. Rather than engaging in a strained human effort to pray constantly, a task beyond human capacity, mystics learn to let God be the beginning, middle, and end of their unceasing prayer.

God is perpetually present to us in the present. The more mystics wake up to the present, the more they are alive to God. And the more they are alive to God, the more their hearts are drawn into his heart; that is, the more they are united to God in a real communion. As this begins to happen, we find ourselves in an ongoing communication and communion with God. As Brother Lawrence taught us, "the soul is always engaged in staying in this divine presence."[38] Thus, by living increasingly in God who is present, we begin to realize the scriptural admonition to pray always.

What a joy this is! What a blessing! It is an unfolding gift from God. How blessed we are! We give thanks to God for the gift of prayer.

It is a wonderful blessing to pray. This is just one of the gifts that God gives us. God gives us the desire to turn to him and then the Spirit in us teaches us how to pray.

Ultimately, our best prayer is to turn our heart's gaze toward the good God. How beautiful God is! How full of goodness! When we turn our hearts toward him we are filled with a sense of joy. Why is this God of ours so good to us, we who are mired in much weakness and sin? Nonetheless, we are showered with God's goodness and love.

This is the prayer of mystics: to fix our spiritual gaze upon God and to allow him to pour divine blessings upon us. It is God's delight to give us this gift. God gives us the gift of thirsting for him always. It is his delight to shower blessings on us. As he looks upon us, we turn our loving gaze toward him. God sees in us the beauty of his son Jesus and says, "You are my beloved Son, with you I am well pleased" (Lk 3:22). It is his delight to gaze upon us. It is our delight to bask in his presence.

We see so much bitterness and hatred in the world. How can we respond? We want to tell people to fix their eyes on the good God. Can hatred exist where there is so much goodness? We are all surrounded by so much goodness in God, and yet many are dying a spiritual death. It is tragic that the overwhelming goodness of God is right at their fingertips, and yet they are dying.

To escape from this hatred and bitterness, we slowly fix our spiritual eyes upon God. We let go of the past and future, and we remain in God who is present. Thus, there ensues a steady communion between the soul and God. Whether we are angry or happy, sad or joyful, our steady companion is the Lord.

As this communion grows, the mood of the mystic almost imperceptibly becomes full of joy. Our dampened moods become less intense and shorter. Our angers are less biting and our anxieties lessen in strength. There follows an abiding sense of joy that is hard for the mystics themselves to perceive since they are unaware of grace increasingly filling their hearts.

Brother Lawrence advised us that our prayer should be simply to remain in the presence of God and if we did, we would be showered with the greatest graces:

> This presence of God . . . if practiced faithfully, works secretly in the soul and produces marvelous effects and draws down to it in abundance the graces of the Lord and leads it insensibly to the simple gaze, that loving sight of God everywhere present, which is the most holy, the most solid, the easiest, the most efficacious manner of prayer.[39]

This transforming change to joy is so slow it is imperceptible until one meets people without faith who are likely to be filled with sadness, fear, or anger. We are struck to see the anger that fills their hearts, the sadness that weighs down their souls, and the fear that terrorizes those who have not yet come to live in God. If joy and God's goodness are signs of "heaven," then a terrorized heart and a raging anger may be signs of hell.

We want to cry out with the words of Jesus, "Let anyone who thirsts come to me and drink" (Jn 7:37). Let go of your anger; do not be afraid. Turn your hearts toward the

Son; turn your hearts toward the God who is here among us.

We, for our part, must be dedicated to the Lord. It is our vocation and our joy to live in God's presence. Each day, we are more filled with this presence. Each day we find ourselves basking in the delight of the Father who finds joy in seeing us, his children. It is a beautiful and blessed vocation. We are so blessed to have been called to such a life. As we more and more fulfill our vocation of being present to God and allowing the Spirit to move in us, we find the scriptural admonition coming true, "Pray always." It is a gift to do so. It is God's work. And it is our joy.

thirteen

Praying Is
Breathing

I HAVE COME TO BELIEVE THAT MOST PEOPLE IN THE WORLD ARE slowly asphyxiating. People are not getting any "air" because their souls are not "breathing." To pray is to breathe. And people are not praying, so they are spiritually dying . . . or they may never have actually lived. Unfortunately, they do not know it and thus their situation is all the more dangerous.

To pray is to breathe. No more than the body can do without oxygen can the soul do without prayer, that is, without breathing in God's life. Every mystic comes to understand this truth by experience. It is not that we pray simply because we have a few extra moments or we believe that it would be a good idea to pray. No. We pray because we must. We are like swimmers underwater who, running out of air, swim mightily for the surface. We are desperately seeking air.

First and foremost, as noted in the previous section, we pray always by opening our hearts to the ever-present God. This gives us a constant source of "air," or life. But this is not enough. Mystics regularly dedicate time to breathe God into their hearts more deeply. They pray because it is their joy. In addition, they pray because they must!

Our life comes from God. We all know this. Indeed, most people recognize that God created the universe, perhaps in seven days or perhaps through millions of years of evolution. Regardless, the plain fact is God created and is creating everything.

However, most of us are not actually Christians in the fullest sense. Instead, we are functional deists. Deists believe that God created the world and now watches it from a distance. Deists posit that the world operates solely under its own natural laws and God does not get involved. At best, their understanding of prayer is that it is a communication from us that crosses over the distance between earth and heaven and finds its target in the God above. At worst, deists give up on prayer altogether since God is not about to change universal laws for us.

One cannot be both a Christian and a deist. One certainly cannot be both a mystic and a deist. Integral to Christian mysticism is a bold proclamation that our God is not a distant God. "For what great nation is there that has gods so close to it as the LORD, our God, is to us whenever we call upon him?" (Dt 4:7). The gospels summarize the message of Jesus as a radical proclamation that God's presence is among us: "Jesus came to Galilee proclaiming the gospel of God: 'This is the time of fulfillment. The kingdom of God is at hand'" (Mk 1:15). It is of the very essence of explicit Christianity, which is Christian mysticism, to give witness to the reality of God's presence among us.

God manifests himself directly to us from time to time as lightning splits the sky and flashes down to earth, illuminating everything. But mysticism goes even one step beyond the occasional illumination of a flash of lightning. *Mystics are so audacious as to preach that this God of ours, because of his incarnation in Jesus, is now permanently, intimately and always in communion with us.*

It is impossible to be a deist and a mystic at the same time. At every moment, mystics are filled with the presence and goodness of God. They are living signs of the truth of Jesus' message: the kingdom of God is at hand! Instead of watching creation from a distance, God's Spirit now permeates all of creation. This Spirit is animating all of creation, giving it life, and bringing it inexorably toward its final communion.

Teilhard de Chardin captured this penetration of creation by God in his poem, "Fire in the Earth":

It is done.
Once again the Fire has penetrated the earth.
Not with the sudden crash of thunderbolt,
riving the mountain tops:
does the Master break down doors to enter his own
    home?
Without earthquake, or thunderclap:
the flame has lit up the whole world from within.
All things individually and collectively
are penetrated and flooded by it,
from the inmost core of the tiniest atom
to the mighty sweep of the most universal laws of
    being:
so naturally has it flooded every element, every
    energy,
every connecting link in the unity of the cosmos,
that one might suppose the cosmos to have burst
    spontaneously into flame.[40]

Despite the theological limitations of his writings, Teilhard's thought is permeated with a wonderful mystic vision. Ultimately, every mystical experience is an experience of God's self-revelation. Teilhard dynamically described one kind of manifestation of the essential mystical experience of God's presence in the world. God's Spirit is a flame that has lit up the whole world from within. And this vision is so wonderful and so powerful it almost seems that the cosmos is about to burst into joy-filled flames.

Since we are not deists, we believe in a God who is ever-present. Our prayer does not have to cross the abyss from earth to heaven: Jesus has already done this for us. Instead, prayer is an opening of our hearts to the God who already dwells within us. "Do you not know that your body is a temple of the holy Spirit within you, whom you have from God?" (1 Cor 6:19).

It is God's presence in creation that gives it life at every moment. In a similar way, we must be in communion with God, that is, we must pray, to keep our own spirits alive and to grow in his grace. If we do not pray, we will not live.

Praying is breathing. Perhaps this sounds like a nice sort of metaphor. But I would not want us to underestimate the truth. In the end, our spiritual lives are much more important than the lives of our bodies. These bodies will surely die, and fairly soon. On the other hand, our spirits will live on in a fully transformed human body. If our spirits are dead, no amount of careful tending of our bodies will matter. Then our bodies will die the final death because our spirits have not allowed God's breath to give them life. Jesus told us clearly, "I am . . . the life" (Jn 14:6). The scriptures also tell us,

Without him nothing came to be.
What came to be through him was life,
and this life was the light of the human race.
(Jn 1:3-4)

There is no life apart from God, which is available to us in Jesus. As Jesus said, "Without me you can do nothing" (Jn 15:5). Moreover, the scriptures suggest that apart from him, we *are* nothing.

I say this with a sense of urgency. Pray often; pray always. Prayer is our connection with Life. Time is short. In the beginning we do not realize how important it is to pray. In the beginning we do not realize how critical it is that we open our hearts often so that God can pour his life into us. As mystics move farther down the path, they realize the necessity of prayer because they realize that God is their all. While this is true for everyone, mystics, as explicit Christians, have come to know this truth by experience. They consciously and explicitly live out this truth in their lives.

Every day our hearts yearn for God's breath of life. Every day we gratefully open our hearts and feel the breath of God surging through us. Ahhh, what a wonderful God who gives us life, filling us with his life! Thank God for his generosity to us. Thank God for his air which fills our souls.

So, mystics pray and pray and pray, and they are glad to do so. Prayer is a blessing. Prayer brings us joy. Prayer is breathing. Prayer is life.

fourteen

Munching

on Jesus

JUST AS MYSTICS MUST BREATHE, THAT IS, PRAY, TO STAY ALIVE, they must also eat. They need to take in spiritual nourishment to live and grow. Jesus himself told us very directly where we are to find this food. He said, "I am the bread of life" (Jn 6:35). It is Jesus himself who is our food and thus the manna of our lives. Jesus said, "My flesh is true food and my blood is true drink" (Jn 6:55).

The problem is that we do not take his words seriously. Rather, we so often "spiritualize" and "sanitize" Jesus' words and thus we empty them of their meaning. Mystics are called to bring people back to the raw truth of the gospels. Jesus said he is the bread of life and he meant it. In fact, the Greek verb used in the bread of life discourse

75

in John's Gospel refers to animal eating and is better translated as "to munch" or "to gnaw" (Jn 6:54-58). Thus, we "munch" or "gnaw" on Jesus.

Jesus went on to say, "The bread that I will give is my flesh for the life of the world" (Jn 6:51). Is this scandalous to us? It should be. When Jesus first preached it, many of his disciples were scandalized. "As a result of this, many of his disciples . . . no longer accompanied him" (Jn 6:66). Jesus asked the Twelve if they wanted to leave him too. It was Peter who spoke, "Master, to whom shall we go? You have the words of eternal life" (Jn 6:68). If we try to live without this bread we will die, just as surely as our bodies will die without food.

As mystics travel the spiritual path, their consciousnesses become increasingly aware and awake. Mystics become ever more acutely aware of truths hidden in the scriptures. For example, they begin to know by experience that every breath they take is a gift and a taking in of God's life. They experience that they inhale God's life with every breath. They are so very grateful because it is God himself whom they breathe in. What a blessing to take in this divine life!

Similarly, mystics come to know by experience that it is Jesus himself who is the source of their food and the one who at every moment is nourishing their lives. Jesus gave his life on the cross for the salvation of the world and now it is this very same flesh that nourishes us in a direct way. It is so direct that the mystical Gospel of John uses this crude Greek verb to emphasize our "munching" on Jesus. When we eat his "flesh," we are feeding on God.

The famous, and controversial, fourteenth-century Rhineland mystic, Meister Eckhart, also spoke of us as "eating" God. While his theological writings sometimes contained mystical hyperbole and imprecise, poetic expression, the spiritual fervor in his thought is compelling:

God . . . is the meat of everything that is. . . . And he is hungered for. They feed on him. . . . They hunger, because he is infinite. . . . Therefore, all things feed on [God], because he is totally within; they hunger for him, because he is totally without. . . . This is what is said, "They that eat me, shall yet hunger."[41]

How do mystics "munch" on Jesus and thus "eat" God? There are many ways. First, Jesus is dynamically present in the sacred scriptures, which we call the "Word of God." As it will become increasingly clear in this book and in the lives of mystics, the mystics' book is ultimately the Bible. When all other books have served their purpose and have been cast aside, mystics continue to plumb, ever more deeply, the inexhaustible riches of the Word of God.

Mystics must do more than simply read the scriptures. Eventually, mystics learn to eat them. Mystics feed on this book daily and have the Word of God pulsing through their veins. They feel a sense of life and breath as they ingest the scriptures. Mystics feed on the nourishment of Jesus in the Bible.

Most important, Jesus feeds us in the eucharist. It is in our participation in this "Last Supper" that Jesus becomes uniquely and most powerfully present. When we eat the bread and drink the wine, it is truly Jesus' body and blood that fills our souls. If mystics hunger for the eucharist, it is because they hunger ever more strongly and directly for the bread of life. They have an emptiness inside that only God's "body" can fill. They must take in this life; they must be regularly nourished by God to live. The eucharist is, par excellence, the bread of life and a "munching" on Jesus.

I have sometimes reflected upon the fact that the eucharist is usually not a moment in which mystics experience great consolations or ecstasies. If this is so, it may be that the eucharist is too intimate, too intense a moment of communion with God to be distracted by such consolations. In the eucharist, mystics come in direct contact with the divine presence; he is taken directly into our souls. Thank God for this food! All day mystics feed on Christ in so many ways, but it is ultimately in the eucharist that their hunger is most satisfied.

And when mystics are deprived of the eucharist for whatever reason, it is a great trial. Their spirits are hungering for the bread of life. They are like the people of Israel who wandered in the desert and cried out to the Lord for bread to eat (Ex 16:2-3). And then, through the intercession of Moses, their spiritual leader, God gave them manna from heaven.

As mystics come to know and experience their complete dependency on God for every breath of life and food to sustain their spirits, one might be concerned that this dependency could be a source of fear or anxiety. What if God no longer desires to give us his bread, would we starve to death? If God no longer gave us his Spirit to breathe, would we stop being able to breathe? The answer to both questions is yes; if God stopped providing us with the grace to breathe in prayer and the manna from heaven that is Jesus' body, we would indeed die.

This can be frightening. We realize how little control we have in life. We cannot control whether we are able to breathe or not; we cannot control whether this manna from heaven will be present to nourish us. The prospect of being this fundamentally and completely out-of-control is so very frightening to people that they shun it. They prefer to attempt to maintain control and to grasp onto safety. They struggle to control and sustain their own lives.

But Jesus tells us, "Whoever wishes to save his life will lose it, but whoever loses his life for my sake will find it" (Mt 16:25). *Letting go of the illusion of control and freefalling into God's unknown space is essential in the mystical journey.* There is no getting around this challenge. We must let go of control; or actually, we must let go of the *illusion* of control. It is becoming increasingly clear that we were deluded into thinking we were in control. Instead, we must free fall into God's space and believe, in faith, that he will be there to uphold us.

While mystics experience God often and in varied ways, this does not obviate the need for faith. In fact, the mystical journey rests even more directly on an act of faith. One might think that mystics do not need faith because they already have some experience of God. But rather, this direct experience of the divine calls upon the need for faith more explicitly. Mystics must let go and trust that God will, at each moment, provide the air for their spiritual lungs and the food for their bodies. We must trust him and his gracious providence.

Perhaps this is why so many do not elect to travel the mystical path or if they begin, fail to continue. It is not an easy path. We want to be in control; we want to be God. Ironically, if we were in control, we would starve to death. It is we who are fickle and alternate between moments of generosity and selfishness according to our whims.

Fortunately, God does not withdraw the breath of his Spirit from us; he does not withdraw the food of Jesus. We breathe in his Spirit freely and we feast on the riches of his banquet. God is not fickle. Thank God we are not in control.

In truth, God has a *greater* desire to share his body with us than we ever have to partake of it. Jesus expressed this divine urgency at the Last Supper, "I have eagerly desired to eat this Passover with you" (Lk 22:15). Once again, we are faced with the divine truth that it is God who has a wonderful and ever-present desire to share himself with us. He wants to give us his Spirit; he wants to give us himself in Jesus. If we could catch but a spark of God's desire to partake in this meal, how blessed would we be!

As we walk farther and farther down the mystical path, our confidence in God strengthens as well as our gratitude. We see more clearly the truth that God sustains us at every moment. Instead of being a source of fear, it becomes ever more a source of our confidence and our peace. The Lord is in charge, not us, and we shall never be in want. Rather, each passing year finds us feasting more fully at the Lord's banquet and breathing in more completely the Spirit of life. If this journey makes us increasingly more grateful, it is because we see ever more clearly the overflowing and immense generosity of our God.

"*O Bonitas!*" This was the ecstatic cry of Bruno the hermit when he was overwhelmed with the goodness of God. It must be our cry as well. How good and generous is our God.

fifteen

The Scriptures

Are Our Consolation

A CHRISTIAN HERMIT ONCE TOLD ME, *"THE SCRIPTURES WERE written for our consolation."* He said it slowly and clearly as if he were passing on to me a great truth. Even at the time, I knew he was telling me something very important, but I also knew that I really did not grasp the meaning of his words. Certainly, as we all know, the scriptures teach us about God and about Jesus. Coming to know the scriptures is coming to know Jesus. But what is this consolation of which the hermit spoke?

It has been twenty years since he spoke those words to me. Only lately have I begun to experience for myself, and thus understand, the truth of his words. Indeed, the sacred scriptures *were* written for our consolation and continue to this day as a consoling gift.

As it says in Hebrews, "the word of God is living and effective, sharper than any two-edged sword" (4:12). Unlike other books, the scriptures are a kind of "sacrament," that is, they carry within them a unique presence of the divine. The scriptures are bearers of grace. This grace is the presence of God in Christ.

When we open our hearts and take in the scriptures, it is God who we are inviting in. He imparts his presence, or grace, into our hearts. When God touches us, it is sometimes experienced as a consolation. This is why the old hermit said the scriptures were a consolation; he came to experience God's presence in the Bible.

As noted in the previous section, mystics day after day take in or "eat" the scriptures. The scriptures themselves speak of the Word of God as bread for the soul. In the Book of Amos we read:

Yes, days are coming, says the Lord God,
when I will send famine upon the land:
Not a famine of bread, or thirst for water,
but for hearing the word of the Lord. (8:11)

But it is God's true desire that we be nourished with his word and have an intimate bond with this Word. Jesus said, "Remain in my word." If we do "remain" in his word, he promised that we will "know the truth" and this truth will set us free (Jn 8:31-32). Slowly, as we "eat" the scriptures and remain in Jesus, his words come alive for us, imparting a special blessing and consolation. Sometimes mystics need only touch the Bible and hold it in their hands to feel the presence of God in these sacred words. Simply touching the Bible can impart a consolation.

It is little wonder then that mystics have always cherished and reverenced the Word of God. The Bible is their constant companion and phrases from the scriptures are never far from their lips or their thoughts.

Hasidic Jewish mystics have a similar tradition. Reflecting on what Christians call the Old Testament,

Hasidic masters have said, "God is present in the words of Torah. Enter into the words, speaking them with all your strength. . . . Your soul will then meet God in the word."[42] The same tradition also says, "The sacred letters are the chambers into which God pours his flowing light. The lights within each letter, as they touch, ignite one another, and new lights are born."[43]

Mystics, then, have an increasing desire to take in or nourish themselves on Christ in the scriptures. As mystics' hunger for God grows, they are drawn to an ever-increasing daily diet of the Word of God. In the end, some mystics find that it is their only book.

I recall another Christian hermit who spoke of his early years during which he read many of the great mystical works. This was an important time of formation and growth for him. But, in his later years before he died, he told me that he found such works too "heady." He had difficulty reading them and could only do so with considerable effort. And this effort did not seem to yield much fruit. However, when he read the scriptures, they opened up for him a simple and direct door to the divine. They became his final book.

Indeed, the scriptures are deceptively simple. We see in them a collection of poems, prayers, stories, songs, prophecies, and recollections. They are easy to read and somewhat interesting at times. But as we move more deeply into Christ on the mystical path, it is only this Word that satisfies. Other books may tickle the fancy, engage the intellect, or perhaps move the emotions, but the sacred scriptures fill the deepest centers of our beings, the place where God dwells. It is the scriptures that are true meat for the soul.

It is not uncommon that mystics eventually lose interest in many of the ephemeral delights of this world. It is not that human novels, movies, or other earthly delights are bad in themselves. Rather, their delight quickly fades and fails to satisfy the soul. Mystics eventually develop a taste and a habit for a richer banquet, the riches of God. It is there that they feast. A steady portion of this feast is the sacred scriptures. His Word is alive and it pierces to the heart.

Thus, we take in the scriptures daily, "chewing" them in our hearts. We pray the scriptures for long periods of time, especially the psalms. We come to know that God is indeed alive in the scriptures. It is his word, that is, the Word of God or Jesus, who we meet.

Eventually, we taste the deep riches of God. We feast on the Body of Christ that is real meat for the soul. This rich food is a source of deep spiritual satisfaction and joy. So, we come to experience for ourselves the truth of the old hermit's words, "The scriptures were written for our consolation."

sixteen

Ecstasies Are

a Distraction

WHEN MOST PEOPLE SPEAK OF MYSTICISM, THEY ARE USUALLY referring to special graces such as prophecies, locutions, visions, ecstasies, clairvoyance, bilocating, or other miraculous happenings. As noted previously, that is *not* the meaning of mysticism employed in this text. I call such miraculous happenings "special" graces. While they are not a necessary part of the mystical journey, special graces may indeed punctuate moments in the mystical journey. Nevertheless, it must be pointed out directly and clearly, and reiterated again and again, these special graces are peripheral to the real mystical path.

If special graces occur, we give thanks to God. If they do not, we have added reason to give thanks. Such graces easily lead mystics away from the true mystical journey.

People focus too much on such graces, and it is tempting for beginning mystics to do the same. In fact, it is interesting to note that the Greek word for "ecstasy" is *ekstasis* which can be interpreted to mean "distraction."

John of the Cross not only preached detachment from special graces, he advocated actually *fleeing* from them. In a sentiment typical of mystics, he wrote,

> The pure, cautious, simple, and humble soul should resist and reject revelations and other visions with as much effort and care as it would extremely dangerous temptations, for in order to reach the union of love there is not need of desiring them, but rather of rejecting them.[44]

Regarding ecstasies in particular, John of the Cross suggested that it is only those who have made some spiritual progress but have not yet reached the final stages who are taken up into ecstasy. For these "proficients," as he called them, their weaknesses cause them to be easily swayed by a bit of grace and they easily fly into ecstasy. More mature, robust souls are not so easily swayed and rarely go into such ecstatic states. He wrote, "For in the perfect, these raptures . . . cease, and they enjoy freedom of spirit without . . . transport of their senses."[45]

With such admonitions in mind, one is ready to speak about ecstatic experiences. Indeed, ecstasies are signs that God's grace directly and powerfully affects the human soul. True ecstasies are not self-induced states of human hyper-arousal. True mystical graces cannot be self-concocted and are almost always a surprise to the recipient.

Padre Pio, a famous twentieth-century Italian mystic, had been blessed to receive the stigmata or wounds of Christ. One critic said that these wounds were self-induced by the mystic's intense concentration on the crucifixion of Jesus. Padre Pio responded by suggesting that this man go into a field, meditate on a bull, and check to see if he grew horns.

Unlike individuals who whip themselves into frenzied states, true ecstatic moments are a surprise; their beginnings and endings are beyond human control, and they do not cause violence to the soul. Rather, they raise the soul usually gently and powerfully outside itself and into a profound state of exaltation. In such states the soul naturally is filled with God's joy and focuses its joy on God. A true ecstasy finds its source and its goal in the boundless generosity of God.

As John of the Cross indicated, ecstasies are marked by the human senses being either partially or totally overcome by the power of God's grace. Thus, the person may not be able to speak or move, or may do so only with considerable effort. In some ecstatic moments, individuals may not be able to hear or see. Of course, such moments must be understood as a complete gift and, contrary to popular opinion, are no indication of the sanctity of the recipient. If one takes the words of John of the Cross literally, then such ecstasies might actually be a sign that the recipient has a long way to go.

In the beginning of the mystical path, or even the state of being a "proficient" as John of the Cross calls them, such ecstatic states are likely to be treasured secretly and sought out. In the throes of an ecstasy, it is easy to believe oneself to be very close to the final union with God. This, of course, is a delusion. It is much more likely that, when one undergoes suffering, feels farthest away from God, and feels the most unworthy, true union with God is much closer. A state of humility is a sure sign of God's immanent and personal presence. We recall that Jesus' last moments of life were not spent on Mount Tabor in a transfigured ecstasy, but on the mount of Calvary undergoing the humiliation of the Cross.

The natural human response to ecstasies could be compared to the human response to a class of psychotropic drugs called benzodiazepines, used to treat anxieties. These medications, such as Valium or Xanax, induce a sense of euphoria and the recipient feels

wonderfully relaxed and peaceful. Unfortunately, the
state is artificially induced and the pills are highly addic-
tive. While ecstasies could not be considered "artificial"
since it is God himself who is the active "medication,"
ecstasies are passing states and very spiritually addicting.
Thankfully, God uses this spiritual "medication" sparing-
ly so we do not become too addicted.

Eventually, the soul comes to realize that these special
graces are only gifts from God but not the fullness of God
himself. At some point in the mystical path such special
graces can become a distraction, turning the mystic away
from the path of humility that leads to a more direct and
profound union with God.

It is then that the soul must willingly move beyond
this spiritual milk to the real meat of the journey. John of
the Cross taught us that our steady increase in spiritual
strength allows us to receive stronger graces. He noted
that the graces communicated to those not fully mature
"cannot be very strong, nor very intense, nor very spiritual—which is a requirement of the divine union—
because of the weakness and corruption of the senses."[46]
Weak, corrupted senses easily fly into ecstasies when
touched even by lesser graces from God.

Ecstasies are wonderful gifts from God and signs that
he is near. They encourage the soul and give it a kind of
foretaste of the future state of blessedness. But the matur-
ing mystic eventually comes to leave these graces behind,
searching for the ultimate prize. As we grow stronger and
steadier, we leave behind special graces and seek the
Source of these graces. We seek directly the One whom no
one can fully describe or comprehend. When God asks us
what we would have, our only response must be an echo
of the words of Thomas Aquinas, "Nothing but thee,
Lord, nothing but thee."

seventeen

Flee From

Locutions

GOD SPOKE TO FRANCIS OF ASSISI AND SAID TO HIM, "REBUILD my church." At the time, Francis was in the Church of San Damiano. Francis believed God was telling him to restore the church building which had fallen into disrepair. With his own hands he helped to restore the church structure. But it is only in hindsight that we understand that Francis' life helped to rebuild the church throughout the world which was badly in need of reform and renewal. And Francis' life continues to have a profound effect on the church to this day. Francis naturally interpreted God's words to him literally and thought that God was speaking of the small church building around him. He missed the deeper meaning of the divine message.

When God speaks directly to us in the interior of our hearts, the words of God's message are called locutions. They are words impressed directly into the soul without going through the physical senses. True formal locutions are clear, strong, and unmistakably of supernatural origin. They are burned into the heart and the recipient knows that a presence outside of itself has implanted these powerful words.

Formal locutions are different from divine inspirations. God may inspire a person to undertake a certain project, make a specific decision, or even write a book. But locutions are direct inspirations from God which are impressed in the soul in the form of distinct words. For example, a contemporary of Catherine of Siena, Juliana of Norwich, received locutions which accompanied visual revelations. On one occasion, the Lord showed Juliana "a little thing, the size of a hazelnut." God told her, "It is everything that is made." She was astounded how small and insignificant it seemed. And the voice added, "It lasts, and ever shall last, because God loves it. And in this fashion all things have their being by the grace of God." Twenty years after these "showings," Juliana wrote in depth about these events.[47] She never forgot those words.

Thus, locutions are a grace implanted in the soul. Unlike normal human experiences whose memory fades quickly, these do not fade easily but last for a long time and carry a power and sometimes pressing quality to them. This is one aspect of discerning the existence of true divine locutions: their memory remains firmly rooted in the soul long after they were received. In addition, these divine graces sometimes carry an urgency and/or an enduring quality, long after the musings of one's mind have dissipated. Thus, when God told Francis to rebuild his church, Francis, impelled by the power of God's word, immediately went about the task of fixing the church.

The power of God's word, which indelibly imprints itself into our souls and can impel us into action, is reflected in the experience of Amos the prophet:

The Lion roars—
Who will not be afraid!
The Lord God speaks—
Who will not prophesy! (Am 3:8)

The unique difficulties with locutions are twofold: discerning their source and understanding their meaning. First, they can be confused with insinuations from demonic sources or, most likely, they can be the overblown musings of one's own psyche. Many believe that the words formed in their brains have a divine source, but more often they have a very human source. Locutions are rare.

Second, even if the soul does experience true locutions, they are difficult to interpret correctly. As the Scriptures tell us:

For my thoughts are not your thoughts,
nor are your ways my ways, says the Lord.
As high as the heavens are above the earth,
so high are my ways above your ways
and my thoughts above your thoughts. (Is 55:8)

The divine Word has multiple levels of meanings, which cannot be plumbed easily or fully by the human mind. Locutions are not simply human words given to the soul, but rather divine revelations that carry within them a profundity of power and meaning. *The Word itself is alive and carries grace in its message.* As John of the Cross wrote, ". . . a person cannot find assurance in his own interpretation, because he is incapable of comprehending the secret truths and the diverse meanings of God's sayings."[48]

In fact, the recipients of divine revelations tend to interpret them too literally, as Francis of Assisi did. John of the Cross wrote:

Souls are misled by imparting to God's locutions and revelations a literal interpretation. . . . God's chief objective in conferring these revelations is to

express and impart the elusive, spiritual meaning
contained in the words.[49]

It is only with the passage of time that the recipient of
these words can begin to understand their meaning. The
fullness of the meaning of God's words may even be
reserved for future generations. And, like all of God's Word,
its depths can never be fully plumbed or exhausted.[50]

What should the recipient of possible locutions do?
John of the Cross rightly advises us to seek wise counsel
from a trained spiritual director:

> It should be kept in mind that a person must never
> follow his own opinion, nor do or admit anything
> told to him through these locutions without ample
> advice and counsel from another.[51]

Moreover, I believe that it is not usually important
for the recipient to try so very hard to interpret the specific meaning of divine communications. The true
depth and meaning of locutions are often beyond initial interpretation. But God's will is not a guessing
game. God does not keep us always incapable of divin-
ing fully his will. Rather, the locutions themselves
carry the power of God's grace which, if the soul only
tries to cooperate, however feebly, will propel the individual down the proper path. It is not for the mystic to
interpret the locutions so much as to receive them in a
spirit of receptivity and to allow God to lead. Francis
never intended to rebuild the entire church, but it was
the power of divine grace in him which accomplished
such a marvelous work. The proper and best response
to any special grace is an act of trust in God.

Mystical graces unfold over time. They are *not* like a
morning dew which quickly evaporates in the rising sun.
It is true that the immediate and often consoling experience of the grace quickly passes. *However, mystical graces
are imbedded in the soul like mustard seeds that grow to an
abundant maturity and reveal themselves over time.*

It is much too easy for those on the mystical path to become obsessed with special graces, particularly locutions and other unusual revelations. It is possible that words, although of supernatural origin, come from demonic sources, with a damning potential. It is more likely that one will be deluded by the ramblings of one's own psyche. And even if the locutions come from a divine source, they are difficult to interpret.

John of the Cross advises us:

The safest and most suitable method of procedure is to oblige souls to flee prudently from these supernatural occurrences, and to accustom them, as we have pointed out, to purity of spirit in dark faith— the means toward union.[52]

Years ago, I would not have thought that John of the Cross's advice was the best. It seemed a bit extreme in its negative characterization of special graces. But, I have come to realize the wisdom of his advice. Special graces are easily misinterpreted, overrated, and are of secondary concern. Should the individual focus on such graces, they are more likely to cause harm than good.

Sitting in the silence of one's heart, and resting in God's presence, is more satisfying and of greater import than any special grace. The mystical journey is most real when it involves an inner silence, keeping vigil in the darkness, and a constant openness to the divine presence. Locutions, ecstasies, revelations, and other unusual graces are often a distraction. If God grants them, one should, with the help of an experienced director, pay some limited attention. However, special graces are not to be sought out and, in the end, should be largely ignored.

Contrary to expectation, the core of the mystical life is not special revelations. Rather, mystics are those whose very source of life comes from God and flows back into God. Mystics feed on God to stay alive and at every moment breathe in the divine Spirit. Mystics do not hear God speaking to them; rather, they become one with the

God who continually breathes forth his Word. The divine Word becomes their Word and mystics eventually realize that it is the heart of Christ that beats within their breasts.

When we understand the mystical journey from this perspective, we see how pale special graces are. They are not really much of a blessing, if any at all. May God spare us from such "interesting" graces and feed us only with his life.

eighteen

Seek Mercy,
Not Suffering

NO ONE LIKES TO SUFFER, AT LEAST, THE PSYCHOLOGICALLY healthy do not enjoy it. It is a masochistic perversion to seek out suffering as something in itself pleasurable. We even hear Jesus in the Garden of Gethsemani praying to his Father, "If it is possible, let this cup pass from me; yet, not as I will, but as you will" (Mt 26:39). Suffering is not something that we enjoy or seek for itself.

While the mystic journey, like any life, includes significant moments of suffering, there is often a link made between the lives of the mystics and intense periods of suffering. The scriptures are not silent on this fact: "For whom the LORD loves he reproves, and he chastises the son he favors" (Prv 3:12) and again, to his own disciples,

Jesus asked: "Can you drink the cup that I drink?" (Mk 10:38). Jesus was speaking of his "cup" of suffering.

Indeed, our ultimate example is the life of Jesus himself, of which the cross forms an integral part. If the cross visited Jesus, it will surely visit his followers. Jesus promised his followers that it would: "The cup that I drink, you will drink" (Mk 10:39). The Christian mystic is first and foremost a friend and follower of Jesus.

Some have suggested that God visits unique sufferings, more than the ordinary, on his special friends. It is indeed true that some mystics undergo an extraordinary amount of suffering. However, as we come to know our God more intimately, it is probably not completely correct to say that God directly and personally puts them through these trials. Mystics come to know that this God of ours is pure light and love. God is full of goodness and knows no evil. It is therefore impossible, I believe, for God personally to visit suffering on people. God does not make people suffer; it is contrary to the very nature of God.

Nevertheless, followers of Jesus must drink the cup of suffering. One way that his mystic friends temporarily suffer is coming, as weak people, into the presence of God's overwhelming goodness. It does happen that the presence of such powerful goodness temporarily causes some spiritual pain. John of the Cross noted that when God's light is infused directly into the human soul, which occurs sometimes in the mystical journey, such pure and overwhelming goodness can be experienced as painful. This is so because we are spiritually "impure and feeble" and thus this powerful grace purifies the flawed soul.[53] The soul is then slowly refined in this fire. Eventually, the purified person experiences infused grace as a joy.

The actual cause of this human suffering is not the will of God but it is the result of human sin and weakness. In fact, the ultimate cause of all suffering is human sin and its concomitant weaknesses. Suffering is not the work of

God. Ultimately, all human suffering comes from the disobedience of humanity.

Jesus suffered, although he was without sin, not because God the Father made him suffer. Rather, he suffered because he immersed himself more totally and more completely than anyone before or after him in the human condition. He experienced the depravity into which humanity had fallen. Immersing his divinity in this darkness, he brought to this same fallen humanity healing and light.

Sometimes people mistakenly believe that the life of a mystic is above or outside of the human condition. They imagine the mystic as being in a perfect meditative calm and radiating an ethereal peace. In this false perspective, the mystical life is seen as one that moves farther and farther away from humanity.

It is true that the mystic comes more and more to experience and radiate God's peace. But this peace is not the kind of peace that excludes human suffering, nor does it separate one from the human condition. Rather, the mystic's peace is a spiritual peace that comes from an increasing union with God; it is not the absence of suffering and conflict. *In fact, this spiritual peace often coexists with intense moments of human suffering.* It is this peace, that is, the active presence of God, which helps to sustain the mystic through this suffering.

Thus, while mystics do not seek out suffering for its own sake, they desire to follow the will of the Father, as Jesus did; and they desire to imitate their master's life. Although God does not make us suffer, since he cannot inflict sin or its consequences on anyone, God does permit people to enter more deeply into the darkness to which humanity has fallen.

Instead of fleeing all that is human, mystics necessarily enter more deeply into their own humanity and the human condition. Thus, they are allowed by God to experience their own sins and the sins of humanity in a more direct and intense way.

This should raise cautions. If our suffering fuels a secret spiritual pride or makes us feel sorrier for ourselves, we may find ourselves suffering and becoming the worse for it. We will have become more arrogant or more absorbed in self-pity.

Even more dangerous is the prospect of entering into the depravity of the human condition and finding ourselves unable to cope with it. Jesus was able to face the passion because of his perfect trust in his Father. We should not presume that we have the same spiritual strength to endure such a trial. It would be better for us, and perhaps more spiritually advantageous, to admit our weakness, eschew great sufferings, and throw ourselves on the mercy of God.

All the sufferings in the world borne well do not add up to the spiritual efficacy of the mercy of God. We must continually remind ourselves of the primary rule: salvation and all grace is a gift. God gives it; we do not earn it through suffering.

Mystics sometimes suffer greatly. They do so because, like their master who entered fully into the fallen human condition, they experience their own sins and the sins of humanity. They do not seek out such sufferings, but like Jesus, they endure these trials when God allows it. When they engage in these sufferings in obedience to the Father and in a spirit of trust, these moments can become, by God's design, a moment of grace for themselves and for others. This grace comes from the shedding of God's light in the deepest recesses of sin.

However, mystics should not concentrate on such things; sufferings and evil should not be the focus of their lives. Rather, they focus their eyes on God who knows no darkness, suffering or evil. God is pure light and goodness. With eyes focused on God, they are able to endure such moments and, like the Passion of Jesus, these moments become transformed by the light of God into sources of grace.

Mystics are friends of God. As God's friends, they come to experience him in a direct way. These divine experiences do not impress God's friends with the importance of suffering. Rather, the soul is stamped with an overwhelming and unforgettable knowledge of the mercy of God. It is all-pervasive, simple and pure, and indescribably consoling.

Mystics come to know by experience that everything pales in comparison to the power of God's mercy. We find ourselves bathed in this mercy. His mercy raises us up in our discouragement and brings tears of healing and consolation. His mercy reaches down into the depths of our hells and dissipates the darkness of our sin. Suffering and darkness are inconsequential when compared to the radiant light of God's mercy.

Each and every moment we commend ourselves to God's mercy. It is the source of our confidence. It is the cause of our peace. It is all that matters.

nineteen

Knowing by

Not Knowing

IN THE *FOUR QUARTETS*, T. S. ELIOT GIVES US AN APPARENTLY contradictory and confusing portrayal of mystical knowledge. He writes:

> In order to arrive there . . .
> you must go by a way wherein there is no ecstasy.
> In order to arrive at what you do not know
> You must go by a way which is the way of
>   ignorance . . .
> And what you do not know is the only thing you
>   know. . . . [54]

We read a similar story from the Desert Fathers:

Some elders once came to Abbot Anthony, and there was with them also Abbot Joseph. Wishing to test them, Abbot Anthony brought the conversation around to the Holy Scriptures. And he began from the youngest to ask them the meaning of this or that text. Each one replied as best he could, but Abbot Anthony said to them: You have not got it yet. After them all he asked Abbot Joseph: What about you? What do you say this text means? Abbot Joseph replied: I know not! Then Abbot Anthony said: Truly Abbot Joseph alone has found the way, for he replies that he knows not.[55]

It has been said that the intellect, through its own reasoning, can come to a knowledge of God. Indeed, the mind can, through its own power, deduce the existence of God through knowledge of created things and through intellectual logic. However, this knowledge of God is a most basic acceptance of God's existence and perhaps some rudimentary intuition of God's nature.

A deeper knowledge of God comes to us from intellectual reflection upon previous divine revelation. Through his son Jesus, the resulting sacred scriptures, and through centuries of revelations to holy people, God has made known truths about himself. A deeper knowledge of God comes through intellectual reflections on these forms of divine revelation. Studying God's self-revelation, the mind can learn more deeply the truths about God. Using these divine revelations, people usually employ their intellects and their own rational powers to understand the truths contained therein. They study these documents; they think about these statements; and they mull over the words.

While this intellectual reflection upon divine revelation is right and proper, these intellectual pursuits do not form the backbone of the mystical way. The intellect is greatly limited and cannot plumb the deep mysteries of

God. If a person only learns and accepts what the intellect can grasp, it will eventually and positively prohibit the person from progressing on the mystical path. As the anonymous author of *The Cloud of Unknowing* wrote, "A man may know completely and ponder thoroughly every created thing and its works, yes, and God's works, too, but not God himself. Thought cannot comprehend God."[56] Many people find their spiritual lives stuck at this point because they cling steadfastly to what their intellects can grasp.

In Bonaventure's mystical work, *Journey of the Mind to God*, he affirms the need for the mystic to move beyond the limited powers of the intellect:

> All intellectual operations should be abandoned, and the whole height of our affections should be transferred and transformed into God. This, how-ever, is mystical and most secret, which no man knoweth but he that hath received it. . . . If you should ask how these things come about, question grace, not instruction; desire, not intellect; the cry of prayer, not pursuit of study. . . . Let us then die and pass over into darkness . . . so that when the Father is shown to us we may say with Philip, "It is enough for us."[57]

While these great mystical writers speak of the need to "suspend all operations of the mind," they are not advo-cating a complete disparaging of the role of the intellect in the mystical life. It would be a mistake to so denigrate the powers of the intellect as to place the mystical path in direct contradiction to intellectual pursuits. Some have done this, but it is an error. In truth, the mystical way of knowledge does not contradict the intellect but builds upon it, and finally transcends it. A properly guided intel-lect leads to the beginning of the mystical way. However, if a person cannot eventually give up the "rational con-trol" of the intellect, there is no hope for real progress on the mystical path.

Here we see clearly the pressing need for would-be mystics to develop the virtue of "trust." They must trust God enough to let go of their rational control. They must give up complete reliance on only what they can know through their biological senses and their conscious minds. Mystics must learn to develop their "spiritual senses," that is, they learn to taste, touch, see, smell, and hear on an entirely new level that is just as real and even more powerful than the biological senses.

As mystics experience an increasing closeness, and eventually union, with God, they learn through their spiritual "senses" who God is. It is this loving union that teaches them truly about God. This is the deep knowledge that Maritain spoke of when he used the phrase, "supernatural connaturality."[58] The mystic learns by becoming one with the Other.

Just as this knowledge transcends the powers of the human intellect, it necessarily transcends the ability of human speech to transmit it fully. It is partly this profundity of meaning and paucity of human speech that drives many mystics to silence. In the presence of God, human words become completely inadequate, sounding trite even as they are spoken. Sometimes the only way to reverence the experience of God is to keep silent:

The abbot Pastor said that when brother Zachary was dying, the Abbot Moses asked him, saying, "What seest thou?" And he answered, "Naught better, Father, than to hold one's peace." And he said, "It is true, my son: hold thy peace."[59]

Thomas Aquinas had a similar experience toward the end of his life. He spent his adult life writing volumes of profound theological works, and to this day Aquinas remains one of the great theological minds of Christianity. Even in his theological writings, Aquinas recognized that "Man reaches the peak of his knowledge, when he realizes that he does not know Him."[60] Moreover, in the final year of his life, he had such a profound experience of God that he ceased writing altogether and left his greatest work, the *Summa Theologiae,* unfinished. Thomas said, "All that I have written appears to be as so much straw after the things that have been revealed to me."[61] The power of the mystical experience of God even silenced the mighty pen of the Angelic Doctor.

Letting go of the intellect's control and silencing the mind, mystics move into the "darkness" of the divine presence. It is properly called a darkness because the light of human senses must be stilled. Mystics may not rely on the light of normal human knowledge or any other faculty they have used in the past. It is as if they are groping in the dark, sensing only faintly the Word of God calling to them from some far off place. In obedience and trust, mystics grope ahead in this darkness, not knowing what lies ahead.

The Cloud of Unknowing teaches us: "For it is a darkness of unknowing that lies between you and your God. . . . Yes, beat upon that thick cloud of unknowing with the dart of your loving desire and do not cease come what may."[62]

In the end, this cloud of unknowing teaches us to trust God and to abandon ourselves to him. More important than any ecstasy, locution, vision, or revelation is the trust in God that the soul learns in the darkness. As we let go of our rational control and abandon ourselves to a God who seems hidden in the darkness, we come to know him in a deeper way. It is only in the darkness that we come truly to know our God in this life. *Special graces are not essential to the mystical journey; touching God in the darkness is of its essence.*

In this darkness, we taste a deep and satisfying knowledge of God. In the darkness of God's presence, our hearts rest and the many incomprehensible contradictions of life are resolved. We sit in peace with the mysteries of life and faith. Jesus predicted this moment at the Last Supper when he said to his disciples, "I will see you again, and your hearts will rejoice, and no one will take your joy away from you. On that day you will not question me about anything" (Jn 16:22-23). All is resolved in a wordless peace.

Mystical knowledge is a knowing beyond intellect and reason. It is a knowledge born of a wordless communion. This communion is only possible when the mind is stilled and the mystic dwells in the deepest recesses of the soul. It was a true word that Abbot Anthony spoke when he said of Abbot Joseph, "Truly Abbot Joseph alone has found the way, for he replies that he knows not."

twenty

Safe Harbor

From Evil

THIS LITTLE GUIDE WOULD BE INCOMPLETE IF IT DID NOT mention, at least briefly, the evil one. It has become fashionable in our day to dismiss the real existence of a personal force of evil in the world; at the same time, people seem somewhat obsessed with dark forces and demonic realms. In a culture that dismisses the recognition of evil, it is not surprising that there are some who use fortune tellers, ouija boards, and call on evil powers. All this is upsetting and very dangerous. The Book of Deuteronomy, with good reason, forbids such things:

> Though these nations whom you are to dispossess listen to their soothsayers and fortune-tellers, the Lord, your God, will not permit you to do so. (Dt 18:14)

God has given us this command for our own protection. *There is no reason to invoke such practices and they can ultimately lead down an unintended and dangerous path.*

It is probably not a coincidence that as society loses touch with the divine, it increasingly fails to recognize the presence of evil. When society loses a sense of the goodness and glory of God, it necessarily loses a salutary recognition and appropriate fear of demonic powers. When people cannot see the light, they no longer become aware of the darkness. What remains is a spiritual deadness and a grey existence.

There are some mystics who have been given the terrible grace of experiencing the reality and the power of the evil one. It becomes very clear to them that there is definitely a personified evil loose in the world and that its power greatly surpasses the weak strength of any human being. Mystics learn quickly that they are no match for the evil one. Were it not for their previous experience of God, they would be tempted to fall into despair or worse.

Mystics also learn that it is a mistake to focus one's attention on this demonic force, even under the guise of combating it. Those who rail the most against evil and sin may be their unwitting companions. When people focus their attention on evil, they take their gaze off the Lord. Evil has a way of seducing souls, just as the sirens of mythology lured sailors to their deaths on the rocks. Rather, let us *always keep the name of God on our lips and the countenance of God before our eyes.*

The seductiveness of evil should instill some fear in the human heart. Evil is powerful and cunning. We must not underestimate it. This ultimately brings us back to the seriousness of life and the choice that we make. In the end, we choose life or death; we choose to follow God or we become the slaves of evil. There is no middle ground; we cannot abstain from choosing. God presents himself in a variety of disguises, as does the evil one. We must and we do choose. The choice that is human life is correctly and starkly presented in the Book of Deuteronomy:

I have set before you life and death, the blessing
and the curse. Choose life, then, that you and your
descendants may live, by loving the LORD, your
God, heeding his voice, and holding fast to him. (Dt
30:19)

One would be ill-advised to pray for the grace to
experience directly the power of evil. It would be even
more foolhardy to attempt to fight evil directly by oneself.
The great monks went into the desert to engage in such
combat, but it was the Lord who called them to this fight
and it was he who was their champion. Nevertheless, we
have heard of some who lost their way in the desert. Once
again, the previously cited, rather frightening story of the
hermit Hero, who was deceived by a dark angel, comes to
mind.

We must content ourselves to be lesser lights. We
should have a healthy fear of evil and must not underestimate its presence in our lives. There is no need to experience evil directly; one need only look out at the world to
confirm its power and its presence.

How should we deal with such a powerful and frightening reality? Very simply, we continue to focus our gaze
upon the Lord. It is he who has already won the battle. On
the cross, Jesus himself has defeated the power of Satan.
The battle is won and we become victors too when Christ
dwells in us. As powerful as Satan is, the power of God
completely overwhelms the darkness of evil. Christian
confidence in God overshadows its fear of evil.

In the end, we have nothing to fear. If mystics find
themselves in direct contact with the power of evil, they
must cling with all their might to God, invoking the holy
names of Jesus and Mary. Focusing their eyes on him,
they constantly invoke the holy names until the fury of
the demonic wrath passes. Like ships battered by a gale,
souls that face the power of evil will be cast about but
never lost. Eventually, the storm will pass and they will
emerge unscathed.

By trusting in God, mystics defeat the demonic forces. Recognizing the infinite power of God and our own limitedness, this humility wins the day. John of the Cross tells us emphatically: "All the visions, revelations, and feelings from heaven, or whatever else one may desire to think upon, are not worth as much as the least act of humility."[63] These are important words for all on the mystic way.

The mystical doctor warns against the seductive power of the evil one and teaches us that evil often deceives souls under the guise of doing good.[64] How many people are misled and do evil thinking they are doing what is right. History gives ample evidence.

Mystics are not invulnerable to the deceits of the devil. John of the Cross warns proficients against being duped by the devil's "vain visions and false prophecies." Some are deceived into believing that "God and the saints speak with them" and they even "allow themselves to be seen in exterior acts of apparent holiness, such as raptures and other exhibitions."[65] It is to combat such deceits and to preserve one from spiritual pride that the mystical doctor encourages souls to run from such visions and dramatic revelations. *The mystic's life is a hidden life.*

John of the Cross's primary antidote to the deceits of the devil is humility and obedience. He suggests "obedience in all things" and cites the scripture passage: "Obedience is better than sacrifice" (1 Sm 15:22). This humility can be found in obedience to one's spiritual director or in religious life to one's superior, and to the teachings of our faith.

While not advocating blind obedience, we faithfully accept that God's Spirit works through those in authority. Mystics should be loathe to defy the dictates of their superiors, spiritual directors, and religious discipline or to strike out on their own, forming a religion or way of life that suits their own personal tastes and preferences. More often than not, such endeavors are exercises in human pride and a defiance of obedient humility.

And Jesus taught that those in authority have been given a responsibility to serve. They, too, are to find their secure refuge in humility. As he said:

> You know that the rulers of the Gentiles lord it over them, and the great ones make their authority over them felt. But it shall not be so among you. Rather, whoever wishes to be great among you shall be your servant; whoever wishes to be first among you shall be your slave. Just so, the Son of Man did not come to be served but to serve. . . . (Mt 20:25-28)

Finally, mystics find a sure refuge from evil in their inner "heaven." They come to find a place where the evil one has no access. In the very center of their souls, God alone dwells and the evil one is cast out from this inner "heaven." When one's house is all stilled, one finds an inner sanctum of rest in God. It is here that mystics live and they are safe from all harm.

twenty-one

Our Radiantly

Humble God

IT IS COMMONLY BELIEVED THAT INDIVIDUALS WHO ARE GRACED with extraordinary revelations must be exceptionally holy. People are enthralled with such supernatural manifestations and flock to witness them. Individuals who are recipients of such graces are held in high esteem.

This dynamic can be dangerous, for the adulators as well as for the idols. We recall that supernatural revelations are gifts of God and do not imply a state of holiness in the recipient. While such manifestations attract great attention, we remember that God's most powerful manifestation for the prophet Elijah was not in the strong wind, the earthquake or fire, but in a "tiny whispering sound" (1 Kgs 19:11-12). It was only after experiencing this tiny, whispering sound that Elijah hid his face, because he knew he was in the presence of God.

Would-be idols and adulators are oftentimes confused. Their seemingly supernatural occurrences can be works of the evil one or fits of hysteria in unbalanced psyches. It is not advisable to run after the latest supernatural manifestation or self-proclaimed miracle worker.

As the Desert Fathers tell us:

> To one of the brethren appeared a devil, transformed into an angel of light, who said to him: I am the Angel Gabriel, and I have been sent to thee. But the brother said, Think again—you must have been sent to somebody else. I haven't done anything to deserve an angel. Immediately, the devil ceased to appear.[66]

We do indeed have a grace-filled desire to find and experience God. It is a divine imperative in us that propels our hearts at every moment to seek out our true vocation. We are "children of the light" and even now, as we dwell in shadows, we search for the light. We long to be bathed in the divine light and filled with its radiance.

But instead of finding this light in the earthquake, roar of the wind, fire or other startling displays of supernatural "fireworks," God is most surely found in the least significant of places. Jesus startled us when he spoke of the last judgment. We were surprised to learn that how we treated the least of our brothers and sisters is how we treated Jesus himself:

> For I was hungry and you gave me food, I was thirsty and you gave me drink, a stranger and you welcomed me, naked and you clothed me, ill and you cared for me, in prison and you visited me. (Mt 25:35)

Jesus added, "Whatever you did for one of these least brothers of mine, you did for me" (Mt 25:40). Instead of finding God in supernatural revelations, we are most likely to encounter him in the humblest of circumstances.

In the last section, we noted that humility is a powerful shield against the wiles of the evil one. We practice this humility when we are obedient and we serve the needs of others. In reality, *true humility is a powerful manifestation of God's presence.* This is demonstrated most clearly in the person and words of Jesus. "For the Son of Man did not come to be served but to serve and to give his life as a ransom for many" (Mk 10:45). More than any supernatural occurrence, a radiant humility is a sure sign of the indwelling of God.

A few decades ago, the concept of humility had been distorted to mean a kind of self-deprecation. This sometimes exacerbated the damage in human psyches and was manifested in low self-esteem and self-effacement. These distortions, which some masqueraded as humility, encouraged destruction of an individual's humanity. *But anything destructive of true humanity is not authentic Christianity. Rather, it is in Christ Jesus that true humanity comes to its fullest flowering.*

It is no wonder, then, that current society has, in reaction to these past excesses, encouraged the other extreme. Instead of a human debasement, individuals are now propounding different forms of individual and societal narcissism. Some are proposing theories of self-entitlement and an inflation of the ego to counteract former doctrines of false humility. As with self-deprecation, narcissism is equally destructive of true humanity. Narcissism, as an artificial inflation of the self, is as fragile as an eggshell. It is a thin shell covering an inner fragility, sometimes a bruised, hurting ego which easily erupts into a narcissistic rage. When the narcissist's outer shell is pricked, the fragile ego is exposed and the weakness manifests itself, sometimes in distressing ways.

To rediscover a true understanding of the concept of humility, and thus a true understanding of a healthy humanity, we might begin with the root meaning of the word "humility." The Latin root of humility is *humilis*. It means low to the ground or earth. It implies a kind of earthiness. To be humble means to recognize that one is part of the earth.

Human beings are made from the earth; we are part of creation. We are not God. We are not angels. We have an earthy existence replete with a "messy" humanity. We have blood pumping through our bodies; we need air in our lungs; we are filled with human emotions and passions. We are frail and prone to sickness. We are limited in what we can accomplish. And one day we will die. We are the stuff of the earth.

It is little wonder that human beings strive to rub out all these signs of their humanity. They try to eradicate signs of human limitation; they work as if their capacities were unlimited; and they act as if their lives will go on forever. In so many ways, humans protest against the first of God's commandments: he alone is God and he alone is timeless. We want to be God. We want to be timeless and unlimited. We want to be made of the heavens, not of the earth. Accepting our humanity is not easy. It is not easy to be humble. We do not want to recognize the truth.

There are many ways in which the grace of humility can come to us. *Nowhere is true humility more fully accessible than in an encounter with God.* When we experience God, we come face to face with our own humanity. What comes to mind is the response of the apostle Peter when he glimpsed the presence of God in Jesus following the miraculous catch of fish. Peter fell at the knees of Jesus and said, "Depart from me, Lord, for I am a sinful man" (Lk 5:8). Similarly, the prophet Isaiah glimpsed the holiness of God and cried out, "Woe is me, I am doomed! For I am a man of unclean lips, living among a people of unclean lips; yet my eyes have seen the King, the LORD of hosts!" (Is 6:5). When we experience God, his piercing light reveals to us the truth.

Humility is nothing other than a recognition of the truth. It is the truth that strengthens the inner self and builds up a solid humanity. As G.K. Chesterton reportedly said, "Those firm feet of humility that cling to the earth like trees." And the truth is that we are made of the stuff of the earth. We are finite, limited and mortal. Ironically, when we find our true humility in the earth, it is then that we find ourselves open to the Truth of heaven, and thus to the radiant humility of God.

As we continue on the mystical way, a startling revelation about God comes to light. It is so startling as to seem heretical, if not impossible. It becomes apparent that the all-powerful Creator willingly and gladly makes himself subject to, and the servant of, his own creatures. John of the Cross, in this divine paradox, tells us:

> The Father Himself becomes subject to her [the soul] for her exaltation, as though He were her servant and she His Lord. And He is as solicitous in favoring her as He would be if He were her slave and she His god. So profound is the humility and sweetness of God![67]

This mystical insight is confirmed in sacred scripture: "Blessed are those servants whom the master finds vigilant on his arrival. Amen, I say to you, he will gird himself, have them recline at table, and proceed to wait on them" (Lk 12:37). In the end, if we are to recognize the truth and be humble, it is because God himself is an overwhelming, blinding humility. Nowhere is this truth more manifest than in the person of Jesus. God decided to manifest himself to us and came to us humbly, as a poor man and thus part of God's own creation. Such an incarnation befitted God's humility.

Some suggest that when God comes again, he will be a wrathful, overpowering figure. This may be true. But, in keeping with the divine humility, I suspect God might come again in a simple, merciful way. And I do not believe that he will condemn us. No, it will be our own pride that condemns us. Once again, he will offer us forgiveness. Once again, he will beg us to accept his love and mercy. Hopefully, we will have the humility to accept.

Special revelations do not guarantee holiness. They are sometimes counterfeited, and even authentic revelations are only signs of God's beneficence. The surest sign of God's holiness in a person is a radiant humility.

If we strive for true humility, it is because God himself is humility par excellence. If we are to be able to tolerate the powerful light of God's humility, we must have layer upon layer of our blind human pride slowly burned away by the truth.

The truth is: we are finite, limited, and mortal. We are made of the stuff of the earth. And it is in this lowliness that we discover the true nature of God. *He himself is humility: radiantly simple and blindingly pure.* Teresa of Avila experienced the humility of God, even to witnessing God's obedience to us:

> His Majesty never tires of giving. Not content with having made this soul one with Himself, He begins to find His delight in it, reveal His secrets. . . . And He begins to commune with the soul in so intimate a friendship that He not only gives it back its own will but gives it His. For in so great a friendship the Lord takes joy in putting the soul in command, as they say, and He does what it asks since it does His will.[68]

The astounding truth is that our God is a radiantly humble God. Each day we sit at God's table and he waits on us. Each day he puts an apron on and gives us his life to eat and his Spirit to breathe. Each day God serves our every need and it is his joy.

twenty-two

The Sound of God

THE SACRED SCRIPTURES TELL US: "THE WIND BLOWS WHERE IT wills, and you can hear the sound it makes, but you do not know where it comes from or where it goes; so it is with everyone who is born of the Spirit" (Jn 3:8). The friends of God come to "know" in their hearts the "sound" of God. Having experienced God in their very core, they learn about their beloved and are able to recognize him when he comes. This recognition is not so much an intellectual awareness of God, but a loving "taste" and memory of him. In an ancient text, Diadochus of Photice confirms that the soul "is able to taste the riches of Divine consolation and to preserve through love the memory of this taste."[69]

God touches the soul in a completely unique and unmistakable way. This divine touch resonates in the deepest part of the soul that is inaccessible to any other human experience as well as being inaccessible to the evil one. Of course, there is always the possibility of being deceived by one's own desires or the wiles of the evil one, and thus a constant discernment and obedience to religious authority is necessary. Nevertheless, mystics develop a subjective certainty of the "sound" of their beloved. As the scriptures say, "My sheep hear my voice; I know them, and they follow me" (Jn 10:27).

This is a source of much joy. Our hearts leap up in gladness whenever we hear the sound of our beloved. It is not so much the wonderful gifts that God gives us, although they are indeed treasures, but rather it is his voice alone that stirs our hearts. We recall the heartfelt words of the Song of Songs, "Arise, my beloved, my beautiful one and come! . . . Let me see you, let me hear your voice, for your voice is sweet, and you are lovely" (Sg 2:13-14). And just as lover and beloved in the Song of Songs engage in a game of searching, finding, losing, and searching again, mystics find themselves delighted in being surprised again and again by the many loving manifestations of God.

Mystics do not know "where it comes from" and are, indeed, surprised and delighted by powerful moments of God's presence. "Surprise" is one of the hallmarks of a true manifestation of the divine. This may be because God wants us to learn and relearn more deeply that his presence is a gift that cannot be earned or controlled. Or, it may simply be that God wants to surprise his beloved, just as humans delight in giving wrapped gifts to their loved ones in order to see the joy-filled delight in the recipients' eyes when the gift is revealed. Regardless of the divine motivation, one of the signs that an experience has a divine origin is its unexpected quality.

This is difficult for beginners to learn. When the God of surprises comes to them, they believe that somehow they have contributed to this heavenly manifestation. They may recall the location where it occurred, the types of prayers they were saying at the time, or perhaps the forms of asceticism they were practicing. Later, in times of desolation, they are tempted to return to these places and/or reenact the circumstances, hoping to recapture previous divine consolations. However, it is to no avail.

This can cause discouragement in some, even in proficients. Some feel guilty and assume their own failings caused such desolation. However, if they have not committed serious sin, it is much more likely that the early time of consolations has naturally ended, and the more serious work of finding God in the darkness has begun. This is a difficult transition and one that some are not able to make. John of the Cross teaches us that mystics must strive for a "deepening of their faith and becoming detached, emptied and divested of apprehensions so as to soar to the heights of dark faith."[70]

Thus, even at this later stage, mystics must still learn more deeply the basic rule of the mystical life: God's presence is a grace. It is purely a gift. To learn this rule brings freedom of heart. On the other hand, to insist upon human control and to refuse to let go of this illusion brings much sadness and pain in the depths of one's desolation. The further one travels along the darkness of the night and becomes accustomed to the spiritual "desolation," the more at peace one becomes and the stronger the soul. Paradoxically, the darkness of the night itself eventually becomes a source of nourishment, even joy.

Mystics must learn to accept God's consolations with open hands and give thanks when they come. These same mystics must also learn to let go freely of these consolations when it is time for them to go. Just as we do not know "where it comes from" we also do not know "where it goes." When we become less emotionally attached to these ephemeral consolations and thus less desirous of God's "milk," it is much easier to let go of the idea of human control. It is then that we can become accustomed to the darkness and to develop a taste for this divine "meat."

In addition to being a surprise, our God almost always comes to us "gently." He usually slips into the soul with such harmony and subtlety, that, many times, it is only after he has left that mystics recognize that he has been present. Ignatius of Loyola, a master of the discernment, wrote:

> The good angel touches the soul quietly, lightly, pleasantly, like a drop of water that is absorbed by a sponge . . . The good spirit enters silently, as into his own dwelling, the door being open.[71]

This, of course, is in contrast to the action of the evil one whose presence may initially be pleasurable but eventually leaves a trail of conflict and disharmony.

Catherine of Siena received locutions from God offering a similar insight into discerning the presence of God and the presence of the evil one. Catherine asked God, "When thou, O eternal God, dost honour a soul by visiting her, by what sign shall she recognize that it is truly thou?" The answer was: "The joy that I leave in the soul after I have visited her, and a desire for virtue; especially the virtue of true humility, joined with the ardour of divine charity." On the other hand, the devil "first of all make[s] his presence known by joy but this is followed by sadness, remorse of conscience, and no desire for virtue."[72]

God is able to touch the soul with great gentleness. He comes in harmony because the soul itself was made for him. He created us for himself and the soul's center is his proper home. We are, indeed, "his own dwelling." God comes to us as a friend, as a lover, and as a family member coming home. There is no need for him to knock at the door.

This gentle God leaves behind a trail of sweetness and peace. This sweetness lingers long after he has departed. It is the divine perfume, lingering in the air, which also gives witness that God has been present. There is no other power or force that leaves such a sweetness and peace. Once it has been experienced, it is unforgettable.

Paradoxically, this same gentleness and sweetness has a unique kind of power to it. Experiences of the divine often indelibly mark the soul. Long after common human experiences have faded, divine moments remain. It is as if a gift has been implanted in the soul and remains long after God has departed. Each experience of God forever changes the soul and remains efficacious as only God can be efficacious. Wherever God has been present, goodness is deposited, strengthened, and continues to grow. This is why dreams, when truly inspired by God, remain in the consciousness and can be remembered long after normal human dreams have quickly faded. It is the same with divine locutions: the words are branded on the soul. God's grace does not fade; it grows.

This, then, is the "sound" of our God. We learn this sound by experience and come to recognize the unique presence of our beloved. Even as proficients we are often surprised by his presence, but these surprises cause us delight. We are grateful that our beloved would visit us and bring us gifts. Just as mature adults primarily cherish gifts as a sign of the donor's love, we treasure God's gifts first and foremost because they are given by him. It is God who we treasure and God himself is the source of our gladness.

The sound of God is gentleness and sweetness; it is also the sound of an unmistakable power. Only God can bring together these apparent opposites. The world understands gentleness and it also recognizes power, but it cannot put both together. Our beloved is a gentle and sweet power. He touches us so softly and with such care, and yet he "wounds" us in a way that is unforgettable. As John of the Cross cried out in ecstasy:

O sweet cautery,
O delightful wound!
O gentle hand! O delicate touch
That tastes of eternal life.[73]

twenty-three

The Noisy

Distractions of

Humanity

HAVING TASTED THE FIRST CONSOLATIONS OF GOD, BEGINNERS
in the mystical way naturally want to continue experiencing such wonderful graces. These early consolations are
an addicting encouragement to begin the spiritual journey in earnest. So, neophytes start this journey searching
for the proper environment and conditions to nurture this
mystical life. This is a good and holy desire.

A common, beginning perception is that the mystical
life in general, and mystical prayer in particular, is
increasingly free of distractions. In this perception,

mystics are thought to be people living a tranquil state of mind, free of conflicts and mental wanderings. Similarly, the mystical state is sometimes associated with a life of complete solitude, free from the "noise" of humanity. Thus, in this isolated and quiet environment, mystics are thought to be free from the distractions of humanity and able to listen directly and completely to the voice of God.

With such an ideal and "angelic" notion of the mystical journey, beginners then strive mightily to find such an environment. Some, having experienced strong consolations from God, have abandoned their responsibilities to seek out a life free of the conflicts of humanity. Others have begun an almost compulsive search for solitude, assuming that it is only in complete isolation that the mystical life can flourish.

Laboring under the conception that a distraction-free environment leads one to God, beginners in the mystical way are prone to criticizing and blaming. They may complain that their meditations are being disturbed by the human foibles of others. In community, for example, the coughing of other members during silent meditation, their perceived lack of sincerity in following a strict rule of life, and their gossiping or little neuroticisms are cited as barriers for others, especially for these budding mystics, in finding God. Among the laity, such very human foibles as the sound of crying babies during the prayer services, people arriving late for church, or the seeming lack of fervor of those in the pews or in the clergy, can elicit criticism and resentment by neophytes in the spiritual journey. These sincere seekers of God are distressed that their world is such a noisy place.

Underneath it all, they secretly blame themselves, believing that if they were more disciplined or holier, they would be making considerably more spiritual progress, which they measure by the consolations they receive and their tranquility of mind. They are distressed that their daily meditations seem marred, if not ruined, by constant distractions that press on their minds. These mystics, as

124 WHEN THE LION ROARS

they become more proficient, are distressed to find themselves seemingly even *more* full of distractions and assailed by the weaknesses of others and themselves. The thought often surfaces in their minds: "If only I could find a place far from these distractions, I could finally find the God I seek."

As with all deceptions, there is some truth buried within that makes it appealing and convincing. Indeed, it is true that mystics often have a unique experience of God in solitude. The mystic is called to be "alone with the Alone." At times, the mystical path is a solitary one in which the soul journeys alone in the darkness, traversing through fear and loneliness, and following a voice only faintly heard.

It is also true that regular times of solitary prayer are usually, although not always, important parts of the mystical journey. Those who are sincere in their desire for God should seek out, if they are able, places and times away from human distractions and dedicated to the spiritual life. Likewise, it is well documented that some individuals are called to a formative period of strict solitude before reengaging the world. For example, Paul the Apostle is thought to have spent three years in the desert after being "seized by Christ." Solitude is interwoven in the life of many mystics.

However, a call to the mystical life is not dependent on one's circumstances of life. As previously noted, mystics are found in all walks of life from hermits living in mountain caves to mothers of many children. Would one advocate that the mother of three young children leave her family to follow God in solitude? Clearly, the answer is no. There have been great mystics who have led powerful mystical lives and, at the same time, have been immersed in the noisy distractions of the world.

The common mistake to which we are referring is the erroneous belief that human foibles and noisy distractions are detrimental to the mystical life. It is a natural, and usually unconscious, preconception held by beginners and even by some proficients in the mystical way. And there are more than a few false teachers who propose such an "angelic" existence as the true path. The Desert Fathers made short shrift of such angelic illusions:

It was told of Abbot John the Dwarf that once he had said to his elder brother: I want to live in the same security as the angels have, doing no work, but serving God without intermission. And casting off everything he had on, he started out into the desert. When a week had gone by he returned to his brother. And while he was knocking on the door, his brother called out before opening, and asked: Who are you? He replied: I am John. Then his brother answered and said: John has become an angel and is no longer among men. . . . Finally, opening the door, he said: If you are a man, you are going to have to start working again in order to live. . . . So John did penance and said: Forgive me, brother, for I have sinned.[74]

Eventually, the erroneous belief that the mystical life should be free of human distractions and weakness must be confronted and dismissed. Otherwise, it will cause much needless distress and may lead to disastrous decisions. In facing this erroneous belief, we find ourselves, once again, led back to mysticism's primary rule: grace is a gift. The mystical life is not achieved by wiping away distractions and expunging human frailty. Even in the later stages of the mystical journey, we find ourselves still grappling with this primary rule of the mystical life. Nevertheless, we should not be discouraged. Only when we have finished the journey do we fully and completely accept the truth. *Only in the final days do we let go of our human pride, embrace the full freedom of humility, and rejoice in our utter dependence on God.*

Eventually, we come to realize and accept that it is impossible to wipe away human distractions and to expunge human frailty. In fact, the farther we travel down the mystical road, the more numerous and ubiquitous they seem to become. We become ever more aware of human weakness and frailty, especially our own. The more conscious we become of the goodness and holiness of God, the more we are able to see our own imperfections. The more we taste the simplicity and peace of God, the more we see just how full of useless and worthless distractions our lives have become. As Teresa of Avila wrote:

> Only humility can do something, a humility not acquired by the intellect, but by a clear perception that comprehends in a moment the truth . . . about what a trifle we are and how very great God is.[75]

Eventually, we find ourselves crying out in despair, "Then who can be saved?" The answer comes back most surely, "For human beings it is impossible, but not for God. All things are possible for God" (Mk 10:26-27).

Ironically, once we become more accepting of distractions in life and in our prayer, these distractions bother us less. The more we accept this human weakness, the less it disturbs our inner peace. Teresa of Avila wrote:

> Just as we cannot stop the movement of the heavens, but they proceed in rapid motion, so neither can we stop our mind . . . and we think we are lost and have wasted the time spent before God. But the soul is perhaps completely joined with Him in the dwelling places very close to the center while the mind is on the outskirts of the castle suffering from a thousand wild and poisonous beasts. . . . As a result we should not be disturbed; nor should we abandon prayer.[76]

Thus, as we become less distressed by our mental distractions, we become less focused on the surface levels of our prayer. It is then that we can move deeper and become aware of the God who continues to work in the center of our hearts, even as the surface distractions of the world continue and thus we are beset by "a thousand wild and poisonous beasts."

Similarly, the more we make peace with our frail humanity, the more this humanity can be an instrument that actually leads us to God. It must be said that we do not use this acceptance of human frailty to justify sin. But we do find ourselves beset by temptation, constantly falling into imperfection. As Paul the Apostle lamented,

> The willing is ready at hand, but doing the good is not. For I do not do the good I want, but I do the evil I do not want. . . . Who will deliver me from this mortal body? Thanks be to God through Jesus Christ our Lord. (Rom 7:18-19, 24, 25)

It is this constant failure to find holiness in ourselves that leads us again and again to rely only on the holiness of God.

Mystics long for perfect solitude and a silence free of human weakness and distraction. This is a holy longing. It would almost always be a mistake to interpret such a longing as a call to criticize one's surroundings and peers, and to strike out in search of a more perfect solitude. There are some who are called to just such a life, but their vocation is rare. Others are called to a hermit's solitude, but only for a limited time of formation. For others, the desire to leave one's obligations in a search for solitude is a misinterpretation of a holy longing that is integral to the mystical way.

We all have a desire for perfect solitude and a mystical silence. Ultimately, it is a manifestation of the desire for God that burns ever more intensely in the heart of the mystic. *God alone is the solitude for which we seek; it is he whose perfection is a silence full of peace.* Sometimes a physical aloneness and a time apart from others can be a help to opening ourselves to this solitary, silent God. But most often we find this God of ours in our distracted human life. It is the noise of humanity that finally helps us hear the silence of God.

Once we have divested ourselves of our illusion that human frailty and the noise of humanity is a detriment to the mystical life, we find ourselves much more at peace. Ironically, once we accept that mental distractions will always be a part of our prayer, these distractions lose their power to hinder the soul from mental tranquility and from its centeredness in God.

We want to flee from our messy, noisy humanity. We want the pure life of the angels. But God has made us flesh. It is a reality we cannot escape. It is only in and through this messy humanity, a humanity that God deeply loves, that the mystic path leads the soul to God.

twenty-four

Bearer of

God's Joy

"SANCTITY" CONJURES UP IN MANY MINDS A KIND OF DOUR, penitential existence devoid of any human consolation. Holy people are often portrayed in the popular media as gaunt, humorless, and fanatical. It is little wonder that Augustine of Hippo, struggling with his conversion to Christianity, prayed for the grace to change his life, but added, "not just yet." All of us want to be holy, but we are afraid of the price. In our search for holiness, we suppose that we will be forced to sacrifice human fulfillment and joy.

It is true that Christianity in general, and the mystical life most explicitly, demands a total gift of self. It can never be a part-time endeavor, reserved for one day of the week or treated as one part of good health like weekly exercise or a balanced diet. There are no part-time mystics and, in truth, no part-time Christians. Christianity demands a total, radical, personal commitment.

When asked about paying taxes, Jesus said, "Then repay to Caesar what belongs to Caesar and to God what belongs to God" (Lk 20:25). Hidden in Jesus' response, masterfully lingering underneath his words, is a well-known religious truth: *all things belong to God*. While the Jewish people of Jesus' day paid taxes to the government, a core religious truth then, and now, is that all of creation belongs to God. The life of the mystic bears explicit witness to this fact and thus renders all things to God.

Mystics recognize that everything must be given back to God. The world fears such a total self-sacrifice and any taskmaster who would exact it. And if God is like us, then this exorbitant tax would rob humanity of all that it is and has. Then mystics, having given up all to serve God, become the poorest of people and the sad creatures that the world supposes them to be.

Ironically, the truth is just the opposite. As Jesus instructed us, "Whoever seeks to preserve his life will lose it, but whoever loses it will save it" (Lk 17:33). Fear propels people backwards into the very object that they fear. In this case, fear of losing one's humanity and very self can cause one to grasp onto it all the more tightly, and thus lose it altogether in the end.

It is the world itself, clinging to its possessions and control, which is being weighed down by a dark sadness. Our world, estranged from God, is in danger of being mired in the very darkness that it fears. What is most frightening is that humanity has fallen so far that it is unaware of its plight; it is not aware of the muck of sadness in which it is mired.

I spent several months on retreat with the Carthusian monks; they are hermits who live an austere life of prayer and solitude. After finishing up my days with them, I returned to the world. Riding on a public bus, I was immediately struck with the pervasive sadness that surrounded and permeated the people on the bus. They were heavily weighed down by their joyless world. The saddest thing was they did not recognize what they had lost; they apparently believed that their life was "normal." I had only come to recognize this horrible sadness after having experienced the joy exuded by the monks. Their eleventh-century founder, Bruno, described their life as "a peace unknown to the world, and joy in the Holy Spirit."[77]

God meant us all to live in his joy and his peace. When we had lost this joy because of sin, Jesus came and promised us a new gift of God's joy and peace. He said, "So that my joy might be in you and your joy might be complete" (Jn 15:11). Jesus told us clearly that it is his joy we are given. Of course, all that Jesus has comes from the Father, so, ultimately, this joy is a sign of the presence of the triune God.

It is important to make a distinction between *human happiness* and *God's joy*. Happiness is an emotional state that cannot be sustained for a long period of time. Human emotions naturally rise and fall with the circumstances. We are happy when things go well and we are sorrowful when tragedy strikes, as it must in every human life.

It is the great mistake of our modern era to make human happiness, as I have defined it, our goal. People grasp for this ephemeral state of happiness and find it always fleeting. They are like Tantalus of Greek mythology who was doomed to stand forever in water that receded when he tried to drink and beneath fruit branches he never could reach. If our human lives are a direct search for our own happiness, it will always remain elusive and just beyond our reach.

On the other hand, Jesus gives us, freely and without restraint, the fullness of God's joy. Closely allied with God's joy is the presence of peace. As it says in Romans: "For the Kingdom of God is not a matter of food and drink, but of righteousness, peace, and joy in the holy Spirit" (Rom 14:17). In the scriptures, peace is not an absence of conflict, but the sign of a profound inner reconciliation with one's self and with God. Like joy, peace is also a gift from God and a sign of his presence.

Certainly, mystics' lives do not preclude human conflict and, many times, their witness places them in direct confrontation with the world around them. But their hearts rest in an unshakeable confidence and peace. Jesus assured them, "Peace I leave with you; my peace I give to you. Not as the world gives do I give it to you" (Jn 14:27). The mystical way is permeated with this wonderful gift of peace.

The scriptures tell us that joy and peace are gifts associated with the Holy Spirit. "The fruit of the Spirit is love, joy, peace . . ." (Gal 5:22) and again, "The disciples were filled with joy and the holy Spirit" (Acts 13:52). With such gifts of joy and peace, it is no wonder that the scriptures encourage us: "Rejoice in the Lord always. I shall say it again: rejoice!" (Phil 4:4). *The natural state of the mystic, who is an explicit Christian, is rejoicing in the Lord.*

However, this joy and peace are not talismans warding off human suffering. As spiritual gifts, God's joy and peace can, and often do, coexist with difficult times. While suffering erases one's memory of human happiness and precludes its presence, joy and peace help to sustain mystics during the dark times. The scriptures bear witness to the joy of the disciples, having been flogged as witnesses to Christ: "So they left the presence of the Sanhedrin, rejoicing that they had been found worthy to suffer dishonor for the sake of the name" (Acts 5:41). Similarly, we read in James: "Consider it all joy, my brothers, when you encounter various trials" (Jas 1:2).

There are powerful examples of martyrs who, in the midst of the cruelest of human sufferings, were radiant with God's joy. Perhaps the most striking of examples is the first martyr, Stephen. As he was being stoned to death, his eyes were raised to heaven and he received a mystical vision. Stephen, "filled with the holy Spirit . . . saw the glory of God and Jesus standing at the right hand of God" (Acts 7:55). During his witness, Stephen's face "was like the face of an angel" (Acts 6:15). The mystics give witness that God's joy can coexist, sometimes simultaneously, with the cruelest of human suffering.

Mystics give up everything in the search for God. But this denuding of themselves is only the shedding of another illusion. We, of ourselves, "have" nothing; everything belongs to God and it is his presence that gives everything life and meaning. When we try to grasp onto anything, including happiness, we find ourselves increasingly frustrated and ultimately angry. Like Tantalus, we are frustrated that we cannot grasp what seems so close. Perhaps this is why our present era, grasping for possessions and intent on self-seeking, is so very angry and violent.

On the other hand, the total gift of one's self in the search for God does not end in frustration. The mystic comes to realize and brings to fruition the truth that God is not only within our reach, the kingdom of God is within us. The cause of our joy is the penetrating awareness of God's presence.

Let us rejoice and be glad
and give him glory.
For the wedding day of the Lamb has come.
(Rv 19:7)

It is common today to quote John's gospel and say, "God is love." This is true. But it is equally true to say, "God is joy." When God dwells in us, we not only can say that we rejoice *in God*, we can also say that *God in us* is radiating his joy. So, the one who is the fullness of joy, radiates his joy in and from our hearts.

God is joy. Jesus admonishes us, "Ask and you will receive, so that your joy may be complete" (Jn 16:24). Why will our joy be complete? It will be complete because what we ask for, what every mystic seeks explicitly and all people seek implicitly, is the fullness of God to dwell in us. Ultimately, it is not possessions we seek. It is not power, prestige, or even happiness that will bring peace to our souls. We want God. Our only consolation can be God. We must settle for nothing less.

The mystical journey recognizes this truth. The mystic gives up everything. Thomas Aquinas, the quintessential theologian, knew this well. He could have had anything from God that he wished, and his only request from God was, "Nothing but Thee, Lord." Ironically, it is in this total self-gift that we obtain everything.

The surest sign of an authentic mystic and the hallmark of true sanctity must be in the radiant presence of divine joy. A mystic is a bearer of God and thus a bearer of his joy. Sometimes this joy is so strong in our hearts that only a mere gossamer tether keeps us attached to this earth. At other times, God's joy is a quiet radiance that gently fills every inch of our lives.

God is joy. He dwells in every corner of our lives. Thus, we, too, are "joy" and we look forward to that day when this "joy might be complete" (Jn 15:11).

twenty-five

Bearers

of God

CHRISTIANITY IS ALWAYS IN DANGER OF BEING TRIVIALIZED. IT is disheartening when people relegate it to being simply a moral code or only a series of rules for living. Often it is described as being a long series of "don'ts." Such a limited understanding of Christianity asserts that if we follow these rules, after we die we will live in a state of happiness we call heaven. Summarized briefly, this trivialized Christianity says, "Be good and you will go to heaven."

There is some truth in this formulation of Christianity. There are, indeed, specific teachings and guidelines for behavior which the disciple of Christ should follow. The scriptures give us ample warning that some behaviors are inimical to the kingdom:

Now the works of the flesh are obvious: immorali-
ty, impurity, licentiousness, idolatry, sorcery,
hatreds, rivalry, jealousy, outbursts of fury, acts of
selfishness, dissensions, factions, occasions of envy,
drinking bouts, orgies, and the like. I warn you, as I
warned you before, that those who do such things
will not inherit the kingdom of God. (Gal 5:19-21)

We do well not to ignore these and similar warnings.
Likewise, it is also true that we are "rewarded" with
"heaven" after the labors and trials of this world. We look
forward to that day!

However, such portrayals of Christianity insidiously
sap it of its power and its promise. These portrayals render Christ a moral teacher and our lives are summed up
on a behavioral score card, with us left hoping to achieve
a future, eternal reward.

In reality, it is erroneous to characterize Jesus simply
as a moral teacher. And Christianity rejects any system
that would render God an exacting judge and distant
from the humanity that he loves. Likewise, Christianity is
not a religion purely of some distant future reward.
Rather, the truth of Christianity is *powerful, immediate, and
overwhelming. We are not simply called to be like God, we are
called to be bearers of God. We are not called only to live with
God in a future heaven, we are called to share, even now, in the
very life and breath of God.*

We read in the Second Letter of Peter: "He has
bestowed on us the precious and very great promises, so
that through them you may come to share in the divine
nature" (2 Pt 1:4). We share in the very nature and life of
God. When our souls "breathe," it is his breath that fills
us; when we partake of the Bread of Life, it is his life that
fills our bodies. Our goal is not simply to be happy with
God; our goal is to be filled with God himself and thus to
be "sharers of the divine nature" or "God bearers."

This divine life that God offers to us in Jesus does not
begin after we die. No. It begins now . . . right now; the

now in which God is present to us. Jesus proclaimed it: "From that time on, Jesus began to preach and say, 'Repent, for the kingdom of heaven is at hand'" (Mt 4:17), that is, right now God's presence is breaking into the world and into our hearts. This is hard to believe and very exciting. It is overpowering. Our minds have difficulty in fathoming such an enormous reality. The early Christians called it: "Good News," that is, the "Gospel." What could be better news than to realize that the God of all life and goodness is right now breaking into the very core of our being?

Christianity is not pantheistic. Pantheists believe that everything is God. But, in a certain sense, Christianity could be called "pan-entheistic," that is, everything is in God. While Christians do not accept the bald formulations of pantheism, we do accept a similar truth that all is permeated by God. In Christ, all of creation is transformed by the Word and filled with the Spirit, thus it shares in the very nature and life of the triune God.

In a burst of enthusiasm, a Christian mystic is reported to have cried out, "I am God." Such proclamations are rightly condemned. Taken literally, this is not true Christian mysticism; it is pantheism. We are not God. However, such a cry is very understandable when viewed as a mystical hyperbole trying to express the experience of divine union.

This, I believe, is one of the most important witnesses and ministries of mystics. The lives of the great mystics teach us that the Christian journey is not a series of extraordinary experiences or revelations. Such revelations are passing moments that actually can hinder true progress if not put in perspective. *The true mystical journey is an explicit rendering of the Christian life which, in its essence, is a journey toward union with God.* Teresa of Avila spoke this truth clearly, "The spirit is made one with God. . . . For He has desired to be so joined with the creature that, just as those who are married cannot be separated, He doesn't want to be separated from the soul."[78] More than any human desire, it is God himself who longs to be united with each of us.

Some medieval texts have spoken of the mystical journey as a path containing discrete stages. A common description divided the path into three stages: the purgative stage (the cleansing stage of beginners), the illuminative stage (proficients who begin to taste God more directly), and the unitive stage (when union with God has begun). I have not chosen to use such language explicitly; however, it is implied in this book. In particular, the word "unitive" describes well the endpoint of the Christian life. In this final stage, mystics experience, in the deepest center of their beings, a union with God. This is the end to which we are all called.

As we begin to realize this awesome reality, union with God, any shallow notions of Christianity are shattered. Of course, it is good and essential to follow Christian rules of conduct and to act with charity toward others. No one can really claim to be a Christian without endeavoring to live according to Christian norms. But the truth of our calling is so much, so very much, more.

The question naturally enters the mind: How can God do this? The answer quickly comes: God can share the divine nature with us because of the person of Jesus. It is Jesus who is truly God and, at the same time, fully human. It is in Jesus that this divine union is perfectly realized. Thus, as we share in Jesus' life, as we eat his body and his word becomes part of us, we begin to share in this divine union.

A second question comes to mind, "Why would he do so?" Again, the answer comes quickly: because of his love for us. Only now are we able to use this word "love" when speaking about God. In our world, the word "love" has been so overused and, like Christianity, trivialized. Today, love is often spoken of as being synonymous with "warm feelings" about someone or something. We say we "love" someone when we have a feeling of affection for that person. And we say that we do not "love" that person anymore when these feelings disappear.

However, when we speak of God as love, its meaning is much more profound. Love is of the very essence and definition of God. It is true to say, "God is love." In fact, the words "God" and "love" are interchangeable. And Love is propelled by his very nature to empty himself for the beloved. Love shares everything, gives everything; Love finds its natural fulfillment in union with the beloved.

Christianity is a religion of love. This love must lead to a union with the beloved, or it is not really love. When understood as the union of two equals, such as two human beings, this union makes complete sense. It is natural to think of two humans being united in love. But what about a union between the Infinite and the finite, between the mortal and the Immortal, between a lowly creature and the Author of all creation? This is a startling and, at times frightening, reality of the mystical journey, and of the Christian message. We who are lowly creatures are to be united with God.

Facing such a union, we are naturally afraid that we would become lost. We are afraid that we will lose our identity, as a drop of water loses its identity when it falls into a mighty ocean. This is the image of pantheism: we are all drops of water in the divine ocean. But Jesus said so often to us, "Do not be afraid." In our union with God, we do not become lost. Despite being taken up into the immensity of the divine, we at last become who we really are. In our union with the divine, we realize finally our true humanity.

Because this truth of our call to divine union is so overwhelming and unfathomable, it is difficult to speak about it. Perhaps we trivialize Christianity because the real truth of Christianity is so difficult to bear. It causes us to pause in wonder and at times renders us speechless. Who would ever have conceived such a wonder?

But God's tender love calms our soul. John of the Cross described his experience of this union:

How gently and lovingly
You wake in my heart,
Where in secret You dwell alone;
And in Your sweet breathing,
Filled with good and glory,
How tenderly You swell my heart with love.[79]

We are filled with a sense of awe at the Love who penetrates our hearts. We are amazed at the generosity of
God who shares his very being with us. To this awesome
truth, we can only respond with silence and wonder.

And yet he beckons us to himself:

My lover speaks; he says to me,
"Arise, my beloved, my beautiful one,
    and come!
For see, the winter is past,
    the rains are over and gone.
The flowers appear on the earth,
    the time of pruning the vines has come,
    and the song of the dove is heard in our land."
(Sg 2:10-12)

twenty-six

A Life Hidden
in the Triune God

THE GOAL OF THE MYSTICAL PATH, AND INDEED THE FINAL END
for all Christians, is a loving union with God. It is not
uncommon for Christians that this mystical union would
be a trinitarian experience. Teresa of Avila had such an
experience:

> When the soul is brought into that dwelling place,
> the Most Blessed Trinity . . . is revealed to it . . .
> through an admirable knowledge the soul under-
> stands as a most profound truth that all three
> Persons are one substance and one power. . . . It
> knows in such a way that what we hold by faith, it
> understands, we can say, through sight—although
> the sight is not with the bodily eyes. . . . Here all

three Persons communicate themselves to it . . . for these Persons never seem to leave it any more, but it clearly beholds . . . that they are within it. In the extreme interior, in some place very deep within itself . . . it perceives this divine company.[80]

As noted in the previous section, the gateway to this trinitarian union is the soul's union with Jesus. As Son of the Father and the Second Person of the Trinity, Jesus is consubstantial with the Father and fully divine. As son of Mary, Jesus is fully human with all the attributes of mortality except personal sin. It is critical for the Christian mystic to hold both the full divinity of Christ and his full humanity. Without both, Jesus cannot be the "way" or the "gate" through which we enter the Godhead.

Similarly, mystics cannot complete the journey unless they hold steadfastly to both their own humanity and their call to divine union. A perennial danger for proficients in the mystical way is falling into the error of not humbly accepting, and living more fully, their humanity. In fact, the more progress we make, the more truly human we become. On the other hand, it is important not to set our mystical sights too low. The final realization of the mystical journey is a complete penetration and transformation of all that is human with the personal, trinitarian life of God. For most of us, an entire lifetime on the mystical path will only be a beginning. It is almost certain that this loving union continues to unfold even in the eternity of the next life.

In this unfolding path to divine union, the Son is the gate or the way. Jesus spoke of himself in such words. He said, "I am the way, and the truth and the life. No one comes to the Father except through me" (Jn 14:6) and again, "I am the gate. Whoever enters through me will be saved" (Jn 10:9). Jesus is the gate through which we enter into union with the Trinity.

At the same time, as the second person of the Trinity, Jesus offers us union with himself: "I am in my Father and you are in me and I in you" (Jn 14:20). As the most efficacious means to this union and, indeed, as the real-ization of it, he gave us the eucharist, "Take it; this is my body" and "This is my blood" (Mk 14:22, 24). Similarly, Jesus is the Word and he urged us to "remain in my word" (Jn 8:31). Union with Jesus, the Word made flesh, is our portal to and realization of our sharing in the divine nature.

God "burns" with a loving desire for this union. It is a fervent desire of God and, unhappily, a desire not con-sciously reciprocated with fervor by many humans. Much of the mystical journey is becoming aware of this unfath-omable call to divine union and enkindling in our souls a desire for it. The farther along we are on the mystical way, the more our hearts long to be united with God.

Because Jesus is God, he too burns with a divine desire for union with us, "I have eagerly desired to eat this Passover with you" (Lk 22:15). His love for us and complete desire to share himself with us culminated in his self-gift. This total self-gift was realized in one act with two moments: the eucharist and the cross. They are two moments of the same self-gift: each moment existing in tandem with the other. In his total self-emptying in the eucharist and on the cross, Jesus expressed the fullness of divine love and made it possible for us to become fully one with him.

In his preaching, Jesus described his union with us in images. He said that he is the vine and we are the branch-es. He did *not* say that he is the stem and we the shoots off the stem. No, he is the entire vine, stem and all, and we are branches that form part of him who is the vine. If branches are separated from the vine they die. But when we stay connected to the vine and are in union with him, it is his "sap" of life that flows through our veins. The same sap that flows through the entire vine nourishes each of the branches. We are nourished with the same life that nourishes him.

As we become one with Christ, we are taken up into the mystery of the triune God. His Father becomes our

Father. As Jesus said, "I am going to my Father and your Father, to my God and your God" (Jn 20:17). We can claim, without reservation, that the Father of Jesus is now our Father. Thus we can pray with confidence the prayer that Jesus taught us, "Our Father." And Jesus promised, "I have told you everything I have heard from my Father" (Jn 15:15). Jesus keeps no secrets from us but reveals everything the Father has revealed to him.

Thus, mystics are filled with an unspeakable wisdom. This wisdom is not about science or nature or other things of creation, but rather it is about the triune God. Mystics come to know God through a loving union with him and through all that is revealed through the Son. It is not surprising that this knowledge of God is most fully expressed by reference to the scriptures. Jesus, in whom resides the fullness of divine wisdom, spoke to us by the words and actions contained in the scriptures, as the best possible expression of who God is. Thus, it is fitting and most effective for mystics to find themselves drawn to the scriptures in their own sharing of the wisdom they have received.

As a necessary result of union with the Son and the Father, the Holy Spirit envelops and penetrates the life of Christian mystics. The Holy Spirit is a breathing forth of the loving union of the Father and the Son. Mystics' lives are filled with the Holy Spirit, just as the Spirit descended upon Jesus at the Jordan River. In fact, it is the presence of the Holy Spirit that identifies the Son. "John testified further saying, 'I saw the Spirit come down like a dove from the sky and remain upon him'" (Jn 1:32).

The mystical life is increasingly a life led in and by the Holy Spirit. Mystics should develop a particular sensitivity and devotion to the Holy Spirit. In close cooperation with a spiritual director and in obedience to the scriptures and religious authority, mystics ever more deeply discern the movements of the Spirit.

It has been a vocation of some mystics to sense the movement of the Holy Spirit as it calls society or the church to reform. This prophetic role is a natural out-growth of a life led by the Holy Spirit. The great mystic Catherine of Siena comes to mind. She urged the Pope, who lived in fear in Avignon, to return to Rome. Not long after, in 1376, he did so.[81] She was a bold prophet who, on several occasions, insisted on action. Down through the centuries, other mystics, like Francis of Assisi, have sounded the alarm and called people to conversion from a decadent life. More than a few prophets have first been mystics.

However, such prophetic roles are the exception and should be undertaken with great reluctance. In fact, one should speak such prophetic words only when impelled by God. The prophet Amos is an example. He protested that he was not a prophet nor did he belong to a compa-ny of prophets. Rather, Amos spoke out because God himself had impelled him to preach: "The lion roars—who will not be afraid! The Lord God speaks—who will not prophesy!" (Am 3:8). Without a divine mandate to prophesy, the place of the mystic is most appropriately a hidden silence.

The mystical life is efficacious not primarily because of any prophetic word preached, message proclaimed, or divine wisdom shared, but because of its inherent spiritu-al power. United to the Trinity through Jesus the gate, mystics themselves, in imitation of Christ, are portals of divine grace. Like Jesus, they are doors through which the overwhelming divine goodness can pour out and shower the earth.

The mystical life is a hidden life. It is a life hidden in God. It flourishes best when not exposed to public scruti-ny. Its battles with evil are intense but secret. Its struggles with its own fallen humanity are lifelong but mostly unnoticed. Its increasing inner fullness of the divine pres-ence is largely concealed except when it blossoms forth in a radiant face and a joy-filled smile.

Whether young or old, married or single, factory worker or monk, the hidden lives of mystics spread light and hope in this world. Without such hidden lights, the world might be enveloped in darkness. But there has always been, and will continue to be, such souls whom God has called to be friends. May all who sense a call to this divine friendship, "run" in pursuit of the "one thing necessary." And may those who have journeyed long on the mystical path, and perhaps find themselves a bit weary, find renewed enthusiasm and energy for the journey.

The journey is long. But it is filled with an increasing flowering of the mysteries of the triune God. As we delve more deeply into these hidden mysteries of God, the only appropriate response is an increasing awe and wonder, praise and gratitude, and a reverential silence. Who could have predicted it? Who could possibly describe such wonders? And with each new and more glorious mansion of God revealed to the mystic, there is a lingering whisper in the mystic's heart: the best is yet to come.

twenty-seven

In the End Is

My Beginning

COMING TO THE END OF THE JOURNEY, ONE MIGHT WONDER what the goal looks like. What does the soul, completely united to God, resemble? Or put another way, what should we hope and strive to be like? The images proffered by some mystical texts may not be images one would expect. T. S. Eliot wrote:

> We shall not cease from exploration
> And the end of all our exploring
> Will be to arrive where we started
> And know the place for the first time.[82]

The mystical journey does not take people to a different place. Rather, it brings them back to where they started. They do not become angels; rather, they become more who they already are. They are not taken out of the world but their journey brings them back to the world with their feet planted firmly in the earth. The only difference is that they now "know the place for the first time."

Jesus presents us with two similar images. He admonishes Nicodemus, much to his confusion, that we need to be "born again" (Jn 3:4). Likewise, Jesus puts forth the image of children: "Amen, I say to you, unless you turn and become like children, you will not enter the kingdom of heaven" (Mt 18:3). At the end of our journey, we are to become like what we were when we began. Jesus, like T. S. Eliot, seems to be implying that the key to entering the kingdom is returning to an original state, and yet we are different. We are adults who become like children: simple, pure, hope-filled, accepting. We are born again. We do not find the end; we find the beginning.

The end of the mystical path does not take people out of the world or away from their human condition. Rather, it brings them to harmony with themselves and ultimately with the God who dwells within. Mystics do not become different or special people; rather, they become *real* people. I recall the words of a cab driver who picked up Mother Teresa of Calcutta at an airport and drove her in his cab. He said that she was the most "real" person he had ever met.

A "real" person is a humble person. Pride is a shackle around our necks, constantly choking us, making it difficult to "breathe." Breaking the bonds of pride, mystics breathe the presence of God freely into their spiritual "lungs." They are constantly sustained by the bread of life which is Christ. Their thoughts are never far from the sacred scriptures, which is food for their souls.

Most often, their countenance is joy-filled. Mystics are joyful people. Even though they may go through times of terrible trials, there is an abiding joy and peace in their hearts that is a sure sign of the indwelling of God. Joy and peace are the unmistakable footprints of God. Two great scriptural images of such ecstatic joy are Moses on Mount Sinai and Jesus on Mount Tabor. Regarding Moses:

As Moses came down from Mount Sinai with the two tablets of the commandments in his hands, he did not know that the skin of his face had become radiant while he conversed with the Lord. When Aaron, then, and the other Israelites saw Moses and noticed how radiant the skin of his face had become, they were afraid to come near him. (Ex 34:29-30)

Similarly, Jesus was fully transfigured by the divinity that was uniquely his: "And he was transfigured before them; his face shone like the sun and his clothes became white as light" (Mt 17:2). Perhaps there is no better visual image to describe the final divinization of the Christian than the image of the transfiguration of Jesus. Through our humanity will shine the overwhelming splendor of God. We will be uplifted and transformed by the radiant divinity of God.

Mystics are largely silent about their own spiritual lives. Such a "pearl of great price" is too sacred and personal to be indiscriminately bandied about. But mystics speak about God with an inner conviction and a ready enthusiasm. Having tasted the sweetness and riches of God, there is often an inner compulsion to speak in praise of this wondrous God. Indeed, "The Lord God speaks—who will not prophesy?" (Am 3:8).

While mystics can be very busy in this world and are fully alive to the conflicts and tensions of human existence, their inner gaze is ever more increasingly fixed upon the face of God. It is God whom they seek and it is union with him that is their conscious desire. With their inner gaze fixed upon God, their inner attitude is one of constant prayer. They fulfill the gospel admonition to pray always.

As they pray always, their lives are constant vigils, ever waiting upon the bridegroom to come. Humankind is in a middle era between the two comings of Christ. And thus mystics' lives, while being ever more transfigured by the God who dwells within, never quite reach the end for which they seek. In this life, there is always some human limitation to the mystical encounter with God. Even Moses, the friend of God whom tradition says spoke to God face to face (Ex 33:11), could never really gaze upon the fullness of God. God said to Moses, "But my face you cannot see, for no man sees me and still lives" (Ex 33:20).

Indeed, the Old Testament tradition indicated that anyone who looked directly upon the face of God was doomed to die. For example, Manoah, after a divine theophany, said, "We will certainly die, for we have seen God" (Jg 13:22). There is some truth to this adage because it is only in the next life, beyond death, that we mortals fully realize the divine union to which we are called. It is only in the next life that we can truly gaze unfettered upon the face of God.

In this life, mystics, once having reconciled fully their inner selves to God, are largely free of human ambitions. Such a state naturally brings with it a healthy emotional detachment from possessions and worldly aspirations. If mystics have any aspirations, it is the one aspiration of gazing upon the face of God. We hear the mystical doctor longing for this moment:

> O living flame of love
> That tenderly wounds my soul
> In its deepest center! Since
> Now You are not oppressive,
> Now Consummate! If it be Your will:
> Tear through the veil of this sweet
> Encounter![83]

As mystics move toward the end of their journey, their desire for the fullness of divine union increases. Paul the

Apostle was torn between his desire to remain in this life preaching the gospel and leaving the world to be with Christ:

> For to me life is Christ, and death is gain . . . I am caught between the two.
> I long to depart this life and be with Christ, that is far better. Yet that I remain in the flesh is more necessary for your benefit. (Phil 1:21-24)

Anyone who is psychologically sound has a natural fear of death. But a mystical grace overcomes this fear and allows mystics to long, in a healthy way, for the end of this life. Mystics long for their divine union of love to be consummated fully, which is not possible in this life. Speaking of the great faith of our ancestors, the author of Hebrews wrote:

> All these died in faith. They did not receive what had been promised but saw and greeted it from afar and acknowledged themselves to be strangers and aliens on earth. . . . Now they desire a better homeland, a heavenly one. Therefore, God is not ashamed to be called their God, for he has prepared a city for them. (Heb 11:13-16)

When the end of the journey comes to us, as it surely will, we will give thanks. And then we will realize that our journey into the fullness of God's love and joy has only just begun. In this end, we find our beginning.

Vigil of Pentecost, 2000

Notes

1. John Clarke, *Story of a Soul: The Autobiography of St. Therese of Lisieux* (Washington, D.C.: ICS Publications, 1976), p. 266.

2. Herbert J. Thurston and Donald Attwater, eds, *Butler's Lives of the Saints*, Complete Edition, Vol. I (Westminster, Maryland: Christian Classics, 1981), p. 511.

3. John of the Cross, *The Collected Works of Saint John of the Cross*, trans. by Kieran Kavanaugh and Otilio Rodriguez (Washington, D.C.: ICS Publications, 1979), pp. 298-299.

4. Ibid., p. 298.

5. See Chapter 7 for more on the important role of a spiritual director.

6. Jean-Pierre de Caussade, *Abandonment to Divine Providence*, trans. by John Beevers (New York: Image Books, Doubleday and Co., Inc., 1975), pp. 24-25.

7. John of the Cross, p. 299.

8. Jacques Maritain, *The Degrees of Knowledge* (New York: Charles Scribner's Sons, 1959), p. 338. For more on this, see Chapter 19, pages 100-105.

9. John of the Cross, p. 718.

10. T. S. Eliot, *Four Quartets* (New York: Harcourt, Brace and World, Inc., 1971), p. 29.

11. Teresa of Avila, *The Collected Works of St. Teresa of Avila*, trans. by Otilio Rodriguez and Kieran Kavanaugh, Vol. Two (Washington, D.C.: ICS Publications, 1980), p. 102.

12. Louis Bouyer, et. al., *A History of Spirituality*, Vol. II (New York: The Seabury Press, 1982), p. 412.

13. E. Allison Peers, *The Complete Works of Saint Teresa of Jesus*, Vol. I (London: Sheed and Ward, 1950), p. 50.

14. Otilio Rodriguez and Kieran Kavanaugh, p. 127.

15. Thomas Merton, trans., *The Wisdom of the Desert: Sayings from the Desert Fathers of the Fourth Century* (New York: New Directions Pub. Corp., 1960), p. 40.

16. William Johnston, ed., *The Cloud of Unknowing and The Book of Privy Counseling* (New York: Doubleday, 1996), p. 85.

17. Thomas Merton, *The Wisdom of the Desert*, p. 50.

18. Ibid., p. 40.

19. Ibid., p. 63.

20. Fr. Benedict J. Groeschel, CFR, *A Still, Small Voice* (San Francisco: Ignatius Press, 1993), p. 65.

21. John Cassian, *Conferences*, trans. by Colm Luibheid (New York: Paulist Press, 1985), pp. 64-65.

22. From Baron Friedrich von Hugel, *Essays and Addresses on the Philosophy of Religion* as quoted in Jerome M. Neufelder and Mary C. Coelho, eds., *Writings on Spiritual Direction by Great Christian Masters* (New York: The Seabury Press, 1982), p. 8.

23. *The Cloud of Unknowing*, p. 105.

24. Thomas Merton, *Spiritual Director and Meditation* as quoted in Jerome M. Neufelder and Mary C. Coelho, p. 21.

25. Helen Bacovcin, trans., *The Way of a Pilgrim* (New York: Doubleday & Co., 1978), p. 166.

26. Brother Lawrence of the Resurrection, *The Practice of the Presence of God*, trans. by John J. Delaney (New York: Doubleday & Co., Inc., 1977), p. 85.

27. Augustine, *Confessions* as quoted in *The Liturgy of the Hours*, Vol. IV (New York: Catholic Book Publishing Co., 1975), pp. 1355-1356.

28. Herbert J. Thurston and Donald Attwater, p. 511.

29. Thomas Merton, *The Wisdom of the Desert*, pp. 50-51.

30. *The Cloud of Unknowing*, p. 105.

31. Ibid., p. 106.

32. Augustine, p. 1357.

33. John of the Cross, p. 717.

34. Brother Lawrence of the Resurrection, p. 110.

35. John M. Cooper, ed., *Plato: Complete Works* (Indianapolis: Hackett Pub. Co., 1997), pp. 1132-1134.

36. T. S. Eliot, p. 32.

37. Ibid., pp. 15-16.

38. Brother Lawrence of the Resurrection, p. 112.

39. Ibid., p. 110.

40. Pierre Teilhard de Chardin, "Fire in the Earth," as cited in *The Liturgy of the Hours*, Vol. I (New York: Catholic Book Publishing Co., 1975), p. 1666.

41. Bernard McGinn, ed., *Meister Eckhart: Teacher and Preacher* (Mahwah, NJ: Paulist Press, 1986), pp. 174, 179.

42. Arthur Green and Barry W. Holtz, eds. and trans., *Your Word Is Fire: The Hasidic Masters on Contemplative Prayer* (New York: Paulist Press, 1977), p. 47.

43. Ibid., p. 46.

44. John of the Cross, p. 202.

45. Ibid., pp. 330-331.

46. Ibid., p. 330.

47. Juliana of Norwich, *Revelations of Divine Love*, trans. by M. L. Del Mastro (Garden City: Doubleday & Co., Inc., 1977), p. 88.

48. John of the Cross, p. 171.

49. Ibid., pp. 164-165.

50. For a more complete discussion of interpreting private revelations see Fr. Benedict J. Groeschel, CFR, *A Still, Small Voice: A Practical Guide on Reported Revelations* (San Francisco: Ignatius Press, 1993).

51. John of the Cross, p. 209.

52. Ibid., p. 169.

53. Ibid., p. 356.

54. T. S. Eliot, p. 29.

55. Thomas Merton, *The Wisdom of the Desert*, p. 52.

56. *The Cloud of Unknowing*, p. 54.

57. Saint Bonaventura, *The Mind's Road to God*, trans. by George Boas (Indianapolis: Bobbs-Merrill Educational Publishing, 1953), pp. 44-46.

58. Jacques Maritain, p. 338.

59. Helen Waddell, *The Desert Fathers* (Ann Arbor, MI: University of Michigan Press, 1986), p. 118.

60. As cited in Armand A. Maurer, trans., *Master Eckhart: Parisian Questions and Prologues* (Toronto: Pontifical Institute of Medieval Studies, 1974), pp. 40-41.

61. Herbert J. Thurston and Donald Attwater, p. 511.

62. *The Cloud of Unknowing*, pp. 53, 55.

63. John of the Cross, p. 227.

64. Ibid., pp. 658-659.

65. Ibid., p. 332.

66. Thomas Merton, *The Wisdom of the Desert*, p. 54.

67. John of the Cross, p. 516.

68. Otilio Rodriguez and Kieran Kavanaugh, p. 164.

69. Diadochus of Photice, "On Spiritual Perfection," as cited in *The Liturgy of the Hours*, Vol. III (New York: Catholic Book Publishing Co., 1975), pp. 154-155.

70. John of the Cross, p. 160.

71. Ignatius of Loyola as cited in Jacques Guillet, et. al., *Discernment of Spirits* (Collegeville, MN: The Liturgical Press, 1970), pp. 84-85.

72. Louis Bouyer, p. 413.

73. John of the Cross, p. 717.

74. Thomas Merton, *The Wisdom of the Desert*, pp. 41-42.

75. Otilio Rodriguez and Kieran Kavanaugh, p. 165.

76. Ibid., p. 320.

77. St. Bruno's Letter to Raoul Le Verd, in *Carthusian Way of Life*, unpublished ms. (Arlington, Vermont: Charterhouse of the Transfiguration, 1987), p. 24.

78. Otilio Rodriguez and Kieran Kavanaugh, p. 434.

79. John of the Cross, p. 579.

80. Otilio Rodriguez and Kieran Kavanaugh, p. 430.

81. Louis Bouyer, p. 411.

82. T. S. Eliot, p. 59.

83. John of the Cross, p. 717.

Selected Bibliography

Bacovcin, Helen. *The Way of a Pilgrim.* New York: Doubleday & Co., 1978.

Bonaventura. *The Mind's Road to God.* Translated by George Boas. Indianapolis: Bobbs-Merrill Educational Publishing, 1980.

Brother Lawrence of the Resurrection. *The Practice of the Presence of God.* Translated by John J. Delaney. New York: Doubleday & Co., 1977.

Cassian, John. *Conferences.* Translated by Colm Luibheid. New York: Paulist Press, 1985.

Catherine of Siena. *Catherine of Siena: Passion for Truth, Compassion for Humanity.* Edited by Mary O'Driscoll. New York: New City Press, 1998.

Clarke, John. *Story of a Soul: The Autobiography of St. Therese of Lisieux.* Washington, D.C.: ICS Publications, 1976.

De Caussade, Jean-Pierre. *Abandonment to Divine Providence.* Translated by John Beevers. New York: Image Books, Doubleday & Co., 1975.

Eliot, T. S. *Four Quartets.* New York: Harcourt, Brace and World, Inc., 1971.

Groeschel, Benedict J. *A Still, Small Voice: A Practical Guide on Reported Revelations.* San Francisco: Ignatius Press, 1993.

Guillet, Jacques. *Discernment of Spirits.* Collegeville, Minnesota: The Liturgical Press, 1970.

John of the Cross. *The Collected Works of Saint John of the Cross.* Translated by Kieran Kavanaugh and Otilio Rodriguez. Washington, D.C.: ICS Publications, 1979.

Johnston, William. *The Cloud of Unknowing and The Book of Privy Counseling*. New York: Doubleday & Co., 1996.

Juliana of Norwich. *Revelations of Divine Love*. Translated by M. L. Del Mastro. Garden City: Doubleday & Co., 1977.

Maritain, Jacques. *The Degrees of Knowledge*. New York: Charles Scribner's Sons, 1959.

Merton, Thomas. *The Wisdom of the Desert: Sayings from the Desert Fathers of the Fourth Century*. New York: New Directions Pub. Corp., 1960.

Peers, E. Allison. *The Complete Works of Saint Teresa of Jesus*. London: Sheed and Ward, 1950.

Waddell, Helen. *The Desert Fathers*. Ann Arbor, MI: Univ. of Michigan Press, 1986.

FR. STEPHEN J. ROSSETTI is a priest of the Diocese of Syracuse. He graduated from the Air Force Academy in 1973 and spent six years in the Air Force as an intelligence officer. After ordination, he served in two parishes before becoming Director of Education of the House of Affirmation.

He is author of the Paulist Press bestseller *I Am Awake* and Twenty-Third Publications' *Fire on the Earth*. He is editor of the Silver Gryphon Award-winning book *Slayer of the Soul* and author of *A Tragic Grace*, published by Liturgical Press.

A licensed psychologist, Fr. Rossetti has a Ph.D. in psychology from Boston College and a Doctor of Ministry degree from Catholic University. He is currently the President and Chief Executive Officer of Saint Luke Institute in Silver Spring, Maryland, a residential treatment program for clergy and religious men and women. Fr. Rossetti lectures and gives workshops to clergy and religious in several countries on spirituality, sexuality, and mental health. He has authored many articles and audiocassette tapes on these issues.

Monk and mystic